Eternity Now

Francis Lucille

Edited by Alan Epstein

Truespeech Productions
P.O.Box 1509
Temecula, CA 92593

www.francislucille.com

This edition © 2009 Non-Duality Press
Non-Duality Press, Salisbury, SP2 8JP
United Kingdom

ISBN: 978-0-9558290-8-6

1. Spirituality, 2. Consciousness

Other books by Francis Lucille:
        Truth Love Beauty
        Perfume of Silence

This book is dedicated to all the beautiful beings who have made this publication possible through their labor of love.

Francis Lucille
Temecula, California
2006

Contents

Foreword

We usually identify ourselves with a mixture of thoughts, perceptions, and feelings. This identification with a personal body-mind is deeply rooted in us. The people around us—our parents, teachers, friends, and so on—believed that they were personal entities, and we have found it quite natural to follow in their footsteps without challenging this belief, which, upon closer scrutiny, will be shown to be the origin of all our misery.

If the body-mind is an object, a personal and limited collection of mentations, there must be a witness to which it appears. This witness is usually referred to as consciousness or awareness. If we investigate what we are, it becomes clear that it is this awareness that is precisely what we call "I." Most people identify this witnessing consciousness with the witnessed mind, and in doing so they superimpose the personal limitations of that mind onto consciousness, conceptualizing it as a personal entity.

When we make a deliberate attempt to observe this witness, we find an unusual situation: Our attempt seems to fail, due to the subjective nature of consciousness, and the inability of the mind to recognize something that is not objective; but mental activity, made up of the current train of thoughts and sensations, seems to stop for a moment. Although this "stop" doesn't leave any memories at the level of the mind, this non-experience generates a strong feeling of identity and an ineffable certitude of being that we describe using the words, "I" or "I am." After a while, the ego resurfaces with the thought, "I am this body-mind," projecting

1

once again the space-time limitations of the personal entity onto the limitless "I am." The limitlessness of the "I am" can't be asserted from the level of the mind, but remains with us as an "aftertaste" when the objective world reappears.

Having been informed of the presence of this witnessing background, and having had a first glimpse of our real self, a powerful attraction, which brings us back again and again to this non-experience, is born. Every new glimpse reinforces the "perfume" of freedom and happiness that emanates from this new dimension. As our timeless presence becomes more and more tangible, our daily life takes a new turn. People, distractions, and activities that used to exert a strong appeal to us are now met with indifference. Our former ideological attachments become weaker for no apparent reason. Our focus on investigating our true nature intensifies without any effort on our part. Higher intelligence sets in, deepening our intellectual understanding of the truth and clarifying our ontological questioning. Many personal conflicts and antagonisms are reduced or resolved.

Then, at some point, the ego is reabsorbed into our witnessing presence, which reveals itself as the eternal beauty, absolute truth, and supreme bliss we were seeking. Instantaneously, we are established in the certitude of our primordial immortality. This sudden revelation of our non-dual nature can't be properly described through words to someone who is still under the illusion of the duality of subject and object. Such a person will understand those words in relative terms, as an objective experience. It is the only kind of experience he can conceive.

How is it possible to convey the feeling of absolute happiness to someone who only knows relative experiences? Given any relative experience, no matter its intensity, there is always the possibility of an even more intense experience. But this is not the case when we are referring to the bliss of our true nature. How is it possible for someone who knows happiness only in relation to objects to comprehend the autonomy, the causelessness, of this bliss? How is it possible to convey the non-localization and the timelessness of this unveiling to one who only knows events in space-time; its absolute certitude to one entangled in relative truths; its divine splendor to one for whom beauty is a relative concept?

If we say that our universe, with all its richness and diversity—the apples in the basket, the loved ones around us, the Beethoven quartet on the stereo, the stars in the nocturnal sky—at every instant emanates from, rests in, and is reabsorbed into our self-revealing presence, our words still fail to adequately describe the immediacy of this unveiling.

They fail to do so because they still convey the notion of a transcendental presence from which this universe emanates as a distinct entity, whereas such a distinction is nowhere to be found in this unveiling. Our self-luminous background, which is the common thread of the dialogues in this book, constitutes the sole reality of all that is.

1

The Art of Not Expecting

What can we expect from our meetings?

Expect to learn not to expect. Not expecting is a great art. When we no longer live in expectation, we live in a new dimension. We are free. Our mind is free. Our body is free. Intellectually understanding that we are not a psycho-physical entity in the process of becoming is a necessary first step, but this understanding is not sufficient. The fact that we are not the body must become an actual experience that penetrates and liberates our muscles, our internal organs, and even the cells in our body. An intellectual understanding that corresponds to a sudden, fleeting recognition of our true nature brings us a flash of pure joy, but when we have full knowledge that we are not the body, we are that joy.

How can I perceive in a sensory fashion that I am not the body?

We all experience moments of happiness which are accompanied by a perception of expansion and relaxation. Before this body perception, we were in a state of timelessness, an unadulterated, causeless joy, of which the physical sensation was simply the ultimate consequence. This joy perceives itself. At that moment, we were not a limited body in space, not a person. We knew ourselves in the immediacy of the moment. We all know this felicity without cause. When we explore deeply what we call our body, we discover that its very substance is this joy. We no longer have the need nor the taste nor even the possibility of finding happiness in external objects.

How is this deep exploration accomplished?

Don't reject the body sensations and emotions that present themselves to you. Let them blossom fully in your awareness without any goal or any interference from the will. Progressively, the potential energy imprisoned in muscular tensions liberates itself, the dynamism of the psychosomatic structure exhausts itself, and the return to fundamental stability takes place. This purification of body sensation is a great art. It requires patience, determination, and courage. It finds its expression at the level of sensation through a gradual expansion of the body into the surrounding space, and a simultaneous penetration of the somatic structure by that space. That space is not experienced as a simple absence of objects. When the attention frees itself from perceptions that hold it in thrall, it discovers itself as that self-luminous space which is the true substance of the body. At this moment, the duality between body and space is abolished. The body is expanded to the size of the universe and contains all things tangible and intangible in its heart. Nothing is external to it. We all have this body of joy, this awakened body, this body of universal welcoming. We are all complete, with no missing parts. Just explore your kingdom and take possession of it knowingly. Do not live any longer in that wretched shack of a limited body.

I have brief glimpses of this realm in moments of stillness. Then I go to work and find myself in an environment which is neither royal nor peaceful, and my serenity immediately disappears. How can I keep my equanimity permanently?

Everything that appears in awareness is nothing other than awareness: co-workers, clients, superiors, absolutely everything, including the premises, the furniture, and the equipment. First understand this intellectually, then verify that this is so. There comes a moment where this feeling of intimacy, this benevolent space around you, no longer goes away; you find yourself at home everywhere, even in the packed waiting room of a train station. You only leave it when you go into the past or future. Don't stay in that hovel. This immensity awaits you right here, at this very moment. Being already acquainted with its presence, and once having tasted the harmony underlying appearances, let the perceptions of the external world and your body sensations unfold freely in your welcoming awareness, until the moment that the background of plenitude reveals itself spontaneously.

This reversal of perspective is analogous to that which allows the sudden recognition of an angel's face in a tree, in one of those early twentieth century prints that so delight children. At first we only see the tree. Then, informed by a caption under the picture that an angel is hiding there, we begin a meticulous examination of the foliage until we finally see the angel. What is important is to know that there is an angel, where it is hiding, and to have once experienced the tree change its form and turn into the angel's face, as the image recomposes to confide the secret of the picture to us. Once the way is paved, subsequent reversals of perspective are easier and easier until we see the angel and the tree simultaneously, so to speak. In the same way, once we have recognized our true nature, the remaining distinctions between ignorance and awakening become progressively blurred and yield to the fundamental "suchness" of being.

I am beginning to realize that I am all gummed up in my body. My sensations and my impressions are of being a separate individual.

How does this gummed up feeling manifest?

I feel as if I were hypnotized by my pride and emotions, especially my anger, and by the agitation in my body.

Right. As soon as you become aware that you are hypnotized, the hypnosis ceases.

How is that? This is unclear to me.

Ask yourself who is hypnotized. Inquire deeply. Who is it? Where is it? You will discover that it isn't possible to find such an entity. If you explore your mind and your body, you will find a few concepts that you identify with, like: "I am a woman," "I am a human being," "I am a lawyer." You can also find certain sensations in your body, certain areas that are more opaque, more solid, that you identify

7

with as well. But, when you look more closely, it becomes obvious that you are not this sensation in your chest, nor this thought of being a woman, since feelings and thoughts come and go, and what you really are is permanent. At this very moment, the hypnosis ends. The occurrence of these thoughts and feelings is less of a problem than your identification with them. As soon as you become aware of them, you distance yourself. You are free. In this freedom, you do not locate yourself anywhere. It is important to stay in this non-localization, and not follow the normal tendency to take a new identity as soon as you let go of the old one, like a monkey who doesn't let go of a branch before latching onto another.

You will discover how wonderful it is to live in the air in this way, without hanging on, unattached. In the beginning, it seems a bit strange, although your new attitude doesn't constitute an obstacle to anything. You can still fulfill your functions as a mother or as a lawyer, feel your body, and so forth. In fact, to be nothing, in the air, nowhere, is very practical. It simplifies life a great deal. Don't be content to merely understand. Put your understanding into practice. Try being nobody. Let go of the branches.

Isn't it hard after that to come back into your body and live daily life?

You never were in your body, so the question of coming back into it doesn't come up. Your body is in you. You are not in it. Your body appears to you as a series of sensory perceptions and concepts. You know you have a body when you feel it or when you think of it. These perceptions and thoughts appear in you, pure conscious attention. You don't appear in them, contrary to what your parents, your teachers, and nearly the whole of the society in which you live has taught you. In contradiction to your actual experience, they have taught you that you, consciousness, are in your body and that consciousness is a function emerging from the brain, an organ of your body. I suggest that you question these beliefs and that you inquire into the raw data of your own experience. Recall the recipes for happiness that were given to you by these same people when you were a child: study hard, get a good job, marry the right man, etc. If these recipes worked, you wouldn't be here asking all these questions. They don't work because they are based on a false perspective of reality, a perspective that I am suggesting you question.

See for yourself, then, if you appear in your body or your mind, or if, on the contrary, they appear in you. It is a reversal of perspective analogous to the discovery of the angel in the tree. Even though this change seems minimal at first, it is a revolution with unimaginable and infinite consequences. If you honestly accept the possibility that the tree might actually be an angel, the angel will reveal itself to you and your life will become magical.

Can you speak about living intuitively from the heart?

Don't be a person. Don't be anything. Having understood that you are no one, live according to this knowledge. When the idea or sensation of being a person no longer deceives you, whether you are thinking or not, whether you are acting or not, you live the truth from the fullness of the heart.

At this point, am I in right relationship with myself and with the world?

Oh, yes. You are in right relationship which is that of inclusion. The world as well as your body and your mind are included in your true self. Love is inclusion. Understanding is an intermediate step, but the final destination, the true center, is the heart.

Is the heart the place between this branch and the next, to use the analogy of the monkey?

If you let go of the branch to which you are clinging without catching hold of another, you fall into the heart. You have to be willing to die. Let everything you know slip away, everything you have been taught, everything you possess, including your life, or at least everything that you think at this stage is your life. This requires courage. It is a kind of suicide.

Is it really like that? For example, do you remember the moments that preceded your recognition?

Yes.

Was it like that?

Yes.

Thank you. Before that did you have any idea what was going to happen?

Yes and no. Yes, because I felt the invitation. No, because, up until that point, I had only known relative happiness, relative truth, relative knowledge, and I could not have imagined the absolute, the ineffable. The Self is beyond all concept, all projection. That is why we can't steer ourselves to it under our own steam, and must wait for it to solicit us. But, when it invites us, we must say yes joyfully, without hesitation. The decision belongs to us. It is the only decision in which we truly have a free choice.

One of the reasons I postpone making myself available to the invitation is that I fear my life will be radically changed.

Oh, yes. It will be.

My family, as well?

Your family, too. Everything will be changed.

I am afraid that people will leave me.

I can assure you that you will regret nothing.

Is it possible to have received the invitation and to have refused it?

Yes. You are free.

Will I be invited again?

Yes. Be ready. Be available. You are available when you understand that there is nothing that you can do on your own to get to the King. When you acknowledge your total powerlessness, you become an empty room. As soon as you become an empty room, you are a sanctuary. So the King can enter, take the throne, and grace you with immortal presence.

§

You have said that there is nothing I can do to get rid of this ego that sticks to me.

There is nothing that the person, that fragmentary entity you believe yourself to be, can do.

Does this imply that all spiritual practice is useless as long as I believe in that?

Exactly. A practice that comes out of the idea of being a physical or mental being can't be called spiritual. It is a process of acquisition that takes you away from the real. What you really are can't be acquired because you already are it. The ego is impermanent. It is a repetitive thought associated with emotions, body sensations, and reactions. When you are moved by the beauty of a piece of music, by the splendor of a sunset, or by the delicacy of an act of love, the ego leaves you. In that moment you are open and complete. If you try to improve your ego by practicing various disciplines, like a collector incessantly increasing the value of his collection with new and more sublime acquisitions, you will become more and more attached to it, and end up dissatisfied and living in isolation.

Is this disappearance of the ego gradual or sudden?

You already know who you are. Even someone in whom interest in the deepest reality has not yet awakened knows moments of joy. During these moments, the ego is not present. They emanate from our true being, which is joy itself. Everyone recognizes joy directly. That by which the Self knows the Self is the Self itself. Only being has access to being. Only joy has access to joy, eternity to eternity. What exiles us from the Garden of Eden and plunges us into a frantic search is the erroneous idea that this true being, this joy, and this eternity are not present. The reabsorption of the ego into beingness, which appears, from the temporal point of view, like a letting go followed by a sudden illumination, puts an end to this search and this frenzy.

What brings about this reabsorption?

There is no answer to this question on the level on which it is asked, since the effect is already in the cause and the cause is still in the effect. Like the beggar in the fairy tale and the magician from whom he learns that he is the king's son, certain apparently fortuitous meetings can acquaint us with our true identity. At the announcement of this good news, this gospel, in the proper sense of the word, a profound instinct rumbles at the depth of our being and puts us on the trail which leads to the ultimate. This inner movement corresponds to a veiled recognition of our true being, and the promise of joyous serenity that accompanies it channels desire into an unknown direction. This recognition does not refer to an objective and temporal reality. It is not located at the level of memory or of time. Thus, this grace can't be forgotten. It solicits us more and more often, and each new recognition increases our desire for the divine. Like the wanderer lost on a cold winter's night who, detecting from the red glow through the window of an inn the presence of a fire within, pushes open the door and warms himself for a few moments by the hearth, we enter the sanctuary and rest for a moment in the warmth of the sacred light before setting off again into the night. Finally, when our desire for the absolute overcomes our fear of death, we offer the pretense of our personal existence to the sacrificial fire of infinite consciousness. Henceforth, nothing stands in the way of awakening any longer and it progressively unfolds its splendor on all the planes of phenomenal existence, which, little by little, reveal their underlying non-temporal reality, like the gaze of Shams of Tabriz that, "was never cast upon some fleeting object without rendering it eternal."

How can I overcome my fear of seeing the truth, which is an obstacle to knowing my true nature?

In the first place, be happy that you are aware of this visceral fear, since most people repress and avoid it. As soon as it begins to show its face in a moment of solitude or inactivity, they turn on the television, go see a friend, or throw themselves into some kind of activity. Discovering your fear is, therefore, a crucial first step.

I don't know if I discovered it. Perhaps I simply sense its presence.

Live with it, be interested in it, don't repress it. Adopt a benevolent attitude toward it, an attitude of letting it come, letting it go. Take it for what it is, an amalgam of thoughts and body sensations. Ask yourself, "Who is afraid?" and you will see the fear-thought depart, leaving only some residues of localized anxiety, the fear-sensation at the somatic level. Basically, all of that is just a show of which you are the spectator. Contemplate that, and contemplate your own reactions, your flight, and your denial. The recognition of your denial is the beginning of acceptance, come what may. In this way, you take the stance of the contemplator, which is your natural stance anyway.

So, everything unfolds spontaneously. Fear is your ego; the monster you cart along in your thoughts and body sensations; the usurper that keeps you apart from the joyous realm that belongs to you. See it in its totality. Don't be afraid of it, even if its features are terrifying. Draw the strength to look at it from your thirst for the absolute, for freedom. When you begin to feel it, think, "Come here, fear. Show yourself to me. Make yourself at home. I am out of your reach." The effectiveness of this method derives from the fact that fear is something perceived, therefore limited. The longest snake in the world ends somewhere. Once it is entirely out of the tall grass, seen in its entirety, you are out of danger because it can no longer attack you by surprise. Likewise, when you see before you the entirety of your fear, when there is no part of it that is hidden from you, there is no part of you that can identify with it. It is an object that has become unglued from you. The umbilical cord of ignorance by which the ego is nourished is no longer operational. This phantom "I," no longer being fed, can't continue to maintain itself. It dies in the explosion of your eternal freedom.

Once we have recognized our deepest reality, a memory of that recognition remains with us permanently. We begin to be aware when the ego intervenes and we can train it to keep itself at a distance to allow us to be more and more open to what we are. Could you comment about this?

It is useless to try to train or eliminate it. When you train or eliminate it, who is the agent of this activity?

The ego eliminates itself.

How could that be possible? This attempt, on the contrary, perpetuates it. The ego is an obstacle only insofar as we pay attention to it. Rather than address this search from the negative side, the ego and its elimination, start from the positive side. The recognition of which you were speaking leaves a memory of fullness in you. This memory refers to a non-mental experience. It does not come from the memory that can only record objective elements. If you allow yourself to be guided by it, if you respond by allowing your whole being to be absorbed by its call, the sacred emotion that it arouses in you will lead you directly to the threshold of your timeless presence. Live with this remembrance. Forget the objective circumstances that preceded or followed this recognition and stay with the remembering itself. Love it as your most precious possession and remember that the source from which it emanates is always present, here and now. It is the only place to find it, here and now: not in thought, before thought, before thinking of it. Don't even think of it . . .

Simply let what is be . . .

Don't speak of it. Don't formulate it. Don't evaluate it; the intervention of thought distances you from it. Don't even try. You are still making too much effort. It is useless. Surrender and be what you already are, absolute stillness.

I want to be here today, and I have chosen to be here, but what can I learn in the presence of a master that I can't learn by myself?

Everything you learn, you learn by yourself. I can't learn for you. Every circumstance, every event in you life teaches you. What you can learn by asking this question is that there is no master in the personal sense to which you are referring. On that level, I am not your master. I am simply happy to be your friend. The true master isn't a person. It is our Self, the Self of all beings. Surrender to it, love only it, be interested in nothing but it. I feel its presence vibrating in those who come to me with the pure intention of knowing it, and they recognize this presence in me. One could say that this presence recognizes itself in the apparent other by a kind of sympathetic resonance. The divine in me recognizes the divine in you in the same instant and by the same movement through which the divine in you recognizes the divine in me. Under these conditions, who is the master and who is the disciple? Who is you and who is me?

I am not sure if this is a question. I was sitting here methodically trying to be calm. As soon as you came in, everything suddenly became very still. I felt like a dying person desperately trying to catch my last breath. My first thought was a marvelous feeling of astonishment. Then, I had the impression that each subsequent thought was an effort to escape the silence that was spontaneously invading me . . .

When you are invited like that, you should surrender completely. Don't try to know where you are in all of this. Don't try to control the situation. It can't be done. Even the first thought that takes note of this experience is already too much. It prevents a complete letting go. It is not enough to receive the royal invitation; you still have to go to the palace and taste the banquet that is your destiny. The truth-seeker in you is continuously involved in controlling your thoughts, feelings, and actions. At a certain point, even he will disappear, since he is only a concept, a thought. He isn't you. You are that freedom, that immensity in which the seeker appears and disappears. You are what you are looking for, or, more precisely, that immensity looks for itself in you. Abandon yourself to it without reservation.

To what extent are we free to determine our lives?

As individuals or as what we truly are?

As individuals.

In that case, we are entirely conditioned. Therefore, there is no free will. It appears as though we exercise free choice, but we are only reacting like automatons, running through the same patterns of our bio-sociological heritage without respite, and invariably having the same old reactions, like a vending machine dispensing soft drinks in a train station. As individuals, our freedom is illusory.

On the other hand, at the level of our deepest being, everything flows out of our freedom. Every thought and perception appears because we want it. We can't understand this at the level of thought, but we can experience it. When we are totally open to the unknown, the personal entity is absent. We then realize that the tangible and intelligible universe arises out of this openness in the eternal present. We want, create, and are at every moment, everything in the unity of awareness.

You speak of being totally open to our thoughts and perceptions. How can we receive everything that presents itself to us in the midst of the frantic rhythm of modern life? Is it possible?

Actually, you haven't the choice, because whatever you think, perceive, or do, you are open to it moment by moment. For example, when a thought arises, this thought is spontaneous, isn't it?

I don't see what you are getting at.

You didn't take any action in order to make the thought appear. Even if you made such an effort, this action itself would be another spontaneous thought. In fact, all things appear by themselves in consciousness, which is always in total openness. Consciousness never says, "I want this" or "I don't want that." It doesn't say anything because it continuously receives everything that arises in its field. When you say, "I want this" or "I don't want that" it is not consciousness that is talking, it is simply a thought arising from within itself. Then you say, "I wasn't open" and that is an upwelling of a new thought. The background of all this mental agitation is consciousness, always open, always welcoming. From the moment you are alive, you are open. Openness is your nature. This is why it is so pleasant to find it; one feels at home, at ease, natural. You don't have to do anything to find yourself in openness, aside from understanding that it is your true nature, that you already are there. As soon as you establish yourself in witnessing consciousness, mundane agitation no longer has a hold on you. You understand the process by which it takes over, and through that understanding, you escape it.

You leap into another dimension. Familiarize yourself with it. See the impact of it on your mind and on your body. My words may seem to you mere ideas at the moment, but the day will come when they dissolve in you, and become a living understanding. The question of how to meditate, be open, or be happy will no longer come up because you will realize that you already are meditation, openness, and happiness.

But we aren't aware of it!

Inquire, find out for yourself. See if it is true that you are continuously aware. See if it is true that what you know yourself to be, fundamentally, is awareness. Don't take my assertions as established facts. Question them, and question your own beliefs as well. Also question the notion of a limited, personal consciousness. Live with these questions, and above all, live in the silent openness that follows each question, in the creative "I don't know." Into this openness come answers that modify and refine the initial questions little by little, making them more and more subtle, until they cannot be formulated any longer. Let this residual dynamism exhaust itself in your welcoming attention, until the ultimate answer suddenly springs forth in you in all its splendor.

Last night you used the adjective "uncolored" to qualify awareness. Where does love and compassion appear in this picture?

The words we use to describe the indescribable have to be absorbed on the spot. If we use them out of context, they lose their flavor and we end up in apparent contradictions. A story regarding this comes to mind. A Ch'an master contradicted himself (seemingly) a good twelve times in the space of an hour. Exasperated, a disciple laid bare the succession of contradictions before the amused and benevolent gaze of the master, whose entire response, simply said, without trying to justify himself in any way, was, "Really, how strange and marvelous! I'll never understand why the truth is always contradicting itself!"

I agree. Awareness is inexpressible. Is compassion equally beyond words?

My remark concerned the first part of your question. First we have to find in ourselves the uncolored center that is perfect freedom and absolute autonomy. When, from that center, from that knowing, we cast our gaze toward the beings that surround us, not only do we see their bodies and perceive their minds, but we fly beyond psychosomatic boundaries directly to that uncolored, limitless place that is our common essence; there, where there is no other. From this uncolored center, action can unfold or not, depending upon circumstances. Action that follows from the understanding that we are, fundamentally, one being is full of compassion, beauty, and intelligence. It can manifest other qualities, but it can, when circumstances require, also don the color of compassion. Always in harmony with the current situation, it leaves no traces and frees those it touches. True compassion defies the preconceived ideas we have of it. It can seem strange, inappropriate, even brutal, but it is free, and that is its beauty. It is a tornado of freedom that blows where it will, erasing in its passage ephemeral attachments and false ideas, until only the indestructible remains: the true, the eternal.

What can you tell us about intelligence?

Ordinary intelligence is a cerebral function. It appears as the faculty of adaptation and organization. It allows complex problems to be handled by bringing into play a large quantity of givens. Linked to heredity and to acquired conditioning of the brain, it operates sequentially, in time. This kind of intelligence is responsible for performing math calculations, formulating logical arguments, or playing tennis. Operating like a super-computer, it excels in accomplishing repetitive tasks and may one day be surpassed by machines. Its source is memory, the known.

Intuitive intelligence appears as understanding and clarity. It is responsible for seeing simplicity in apparent complexity. It strikes directly, in the moment. Always creative, free of the known, it is at the heart of all scientific discoveries and great works of art. Its source is the supreme intelligence of timeless awareness.

When intuitive intelligence turns upon itself, trying to grasp its source, it loses itself in the instantaneous apperception of supreme intelligence. The recognition of that higher intelligence is an implosion that destroys the illusion that we are a personal entity.

Does this recognition occur independently of someone's level of general intelligence?

Yes. The presence of an intense desire for awakening is a sure sign that this recognition has taken place.

Is the destruction of the ego induced by a gradual or a sudden awakening?

The first moment of recognition already contains in it the germ of its fulfillment, in the same way that the seed already contains the flower, the tree, and the fruit. For a little while, the ego, stricken by the still partial vision of this intelligence, retains a semblance of life. At this stage, habit still maintains its old identifications, but an irreparable breach has slipped into the belief in our separate existence. One's heart is no longer in it, one could say, in all senses of the word. Intermittent recurrences of this recognition widen this gap even further until the moment when the ego, which is a perceived object, becomes completely objective, prior to dissolving before our very eyes, making way for the invasion of the ineffable.

Following this awakening, we find ourselves free of fear and desire. Free of fear because, having reintegrated our immortal self, the specter of death leaves us forever. Free of desire because, knowing the absolute fullness of being, the old attraction objects held for us ceases spontaneously. Old physical and mental habits that derived from the former belief in a personal existence can manifest for yet a while, but all identification with objects perceived or thought is impossible henceforth.

When contemplated in the amazing neutrality of awareness, these habits die, one by one, without their occasional recurrence triggering a return of the illusion of the ego.

What are the signs by which we can recognize higher intelligence?

Thoughts, feelings, and actions that flow from higher intelligence refer to their source, the self. As they fade out back into their source, they leave us on the shore of the absolute, like the foam that a wave deposits on the sand. The thought that thinks truth proceeds from truth, and brings us back to truth. This thought has many different facets. It poses apparently diverse questions like: What is happiness? What is God? Who am I? All these questions originate from a common source: from eternal joy, from the divine, from our self.

When these questions, permeated by the fragrance of truth, invite you, make room for them, make time for them, surrender to them, let yourself be carried by them. These thoughts are like the footprint of God in your soul. Let it proceed where it will. The one in whom these thoughts have awakened is very fortunate. No obstacle can prevent him access to the truth. Once the desire for the ultimate has grasped you, the entire universe cooperates in the fulfillment of this desire.

Are you in this state of fulfillment at this moment?

There is no one in that state. This non-state is the absence of the person.

Do you go in and out?

It isn't a state.

Are you awake in that state?

This non-state is awake to itself. It is awareness. I am awareness, you are awareness.

In that case, you are aware that everything is in its place?

From the point of view of awareness, everything is awareness, thus everything is in its place. Nothing is tragic. All is light, all is presence.

Given that we are light and that the things around us are also that light, do you see things differently from us?

No. I see everything exactly the way you do, but there are things you believe you see that I don't see. I don't see a personal entity in the picture. Even if an old habit arising from memory comes up, it is totally objectivized. It is simply part of the picture. It is not what I am. I don't take myself as something thought of or perceived. That is all. You can do the same thing. You are free. It is enough to just try. Do it! Right now!

How do I go about it?

Each time you take yourself to be an object, for example, a body or a man with a certain profession, be aware of it.

So there is a self at a higher level that observes the situation. Is that the perspective?

That is the intellectual understanding of the perspective, not its reality. The reality is your welcoming attention, not the concept of your welcoming attention, or the concept of yourself as welcoming attention. It is simply your luminous presence, without tension or resistance, welcoming moment by moment the thought or sensation that is coming into being, letting it unfold freely, and letting it reabsorb into itself without leaving any traces. This original light is not an absence but a fullness. Surrender yourself to it. Let yourself be overcome by it.

2

The Direct Path

When we experience enlightenment, do we have knowledge of our past incarnations? Is this what the Ch'an masters mean when they speak about seeing our original face?

The one who "experiences" enlightenment is not a limited entity allegedly subject to reincarnation. There is only one light, one awareness, in which all times, all worlds, and all incarnations have their being in a timeless simultaneity beyond the grasp of the serial mind. In fact, nobody experiences enlightenment, because it is a non-objective experience in the absence of a personal entity. It could be said that, in this non-experience, our original face sees itself; there all questions find their ultimate answer.

If there is an end to ignorance, there must be also a beginning to it. How could it be "beginningless"? If there is a beginning to delusion, how can I be certain that it won't begin again after it has ended?

Everything that has a beginning and an end originates from, exists in, and merges with this timeless background of awareness. Although everything appears to have a beginning and an end in time, a deep investigation will show that in reality everything, including the notions of time and space, has its origin and its end in our timeless essence: awareness, our real "I." Having its origin and its end in consciousness, such a "thing" is not different from awareness. Its substance is awareness, just as gold is the real nature of a ring. It follows that everything is pure consciousness, pure being, pure bliss. Time and all other objects, as such, are illusions. They borrow their reality from consciousness, but they have no independent existence, and, therefore, no beginning and no end in time.

When you speak of delusion, you implicitly assume that there is a person who is deluded and who will become enlightened at some point in the future. If you seriously inquire about this personal entity, it will turn out to merely be a perceived object, made of thoughts and bodily sensations, subject to appearance and disappearance, totally distinct from the permanent self you intuitively know yourself to be. Who then was subject to delusion? It couldn't possibly be awareness, your real self, the ultimate truth; but, on the other hand, it couldn't possibly be a personal entity either, because such an entity is a perceived object which, being lifeless and non-sentient, can't be deluded. When this is understood, it becomes clear that nobody has ever been deluded. If nobody has ever been deluded, then nobody will, nor can, ever be delivered from ignorance. So, the question of falling into delusion again can't arise at that level. Your question is posed from the illusory level of an ego. It assumes that the ego, which is delusion itself, and the origin of all delusion, can be delivered some day from ignorance. It is ignorance playing with the thought that it can be liberated from ignorance, and subsequently worrying that it may fall again into ignorance.

୬

I keep thinking about enlightenment and wondering whether or not it is a formless state. When you said, a few days ago, that all limitations are perceived, I immediately saw it to be true. I realized that any belief I might have about enlightenment is just another limitation.

Yes, your belief about enlightenment being formless is a limitation superimposed onto that which you are. When you try to imagine happiness or truth, you first try to see it as an object, gross or subtle, profane or sacred. Then, at some point, you begin to think that it isn't an object, so you try to imagine it as a non-object, a void, and you arrive at a blank state which you usually can't maintain (some yogins can). This state isn't the splendor, certainty, and bliss you are seeking. This blank state is often an enigma for the truth-seeker, who can't go beyond it by his own efforts. To do so, the living presence of an instructor is required in most cases. This blank state is still an object. In order to go beyond this state, the mind has to understand that enlightenment is totally beyond its reach. When this is understood, the mind becomes naturally quiet, because it has no place to go. This spontaneous and effortless quieting of the mind is pure welcoming. In this openness lies the opportunity to be knowingly that which you are.

ॐ

Is my constant search for the truth driven by the ego?

I feel that you are seriously interested in the truth, that the search for your true being is the most important activity in your life. I don't mean that you aren't interested in other aspects of life, but rather that your love for the ultimate truth has become the axis around which everything else revolves. If you were told that you had only a few days to live, I am certain that the central question in your mind would be about the ultimate. This should make clear to you where the gravitational center of your desires lies. Such a desire, such a dedicated search, doesn't come from the ego, but from truth itself. You may also feel that when you surrender to your desire for the truth by investigating, by looking for new books, by meeting spiritual friends, you experience a foretaste of causeless bliss. So, I suggest that you recognize your love for understanding, take it as your guide, and surrender to it whenever it invites you. Know with complete certainty that the actions that flow from it are not ego-driven, unlike the fears, concerns, and doubts that arise from the notion of being a separate entity.

Your search for the truth should be totally open-minded, free from any beliefs, or from any intellectual attachment to a specific religion or philosophy. It should be based solely on your intimate feeling of harmony, understanding, and devotion. Contemplate your innate beauty, intelligence, and love as you spontaneously respond to a majestic sunset, a scripture that points directly to the truth, a meeting with a friend who is free from the notion of being a personal entity, or more generally, to any situation in your life. In this way, your investigation remains lively, innocent, and effortless. It will lead you inexorably and joyfully to that background which is the common goal of religion and philosophy.

ℒ

Does the direct path consist in carrying on with everyday life while awaiting grace?

We don't have to carry on with anything. Life carries on with itself, by itself, without our intervention. Everything that comes to us unexpectedly is grace. Why wait for it? Why postpone it? Why fail to welcome it? Simply be open to the possibility that whatever the present moment is bringing to you is a gift from grace. That is the direct path.

I understand that we must already be the ultimate reality, but this knowledge is covered up by ignorance.

Yes. Your use of the word "must" implies that you are drawing a logical inference, which shows that the understanding to which you are referring, that we already are the ultimate, is intellectual. Nevertheless, this conceptual understanding leaves open the possibility that this is actually the case; that we are the absolute, the one without a second. If it is so, what we really are obviously stands beyond the grasp of our limited mind. When we see that the mind, in spite of all its abilities, is absolutely unable to comprehend the truth for which we are striving, all effort to reach enlightenment ceases naturally. This effortlessness is the threshold of real understanding beyond all limitations.

Are you saying that the gradual paths, such as the path of understanding (Jnana Yoga), of right action (Karma Yoga), of devotion to the Divine, or to the spiritual teacher (Bhakti Yoga) are mistaken?

When you understand the truth revealed in the scriptures, where is the ignorance? When you see things as they truly are, where is the illusion? When you act spontaneously in accordance with this true understanding, simply responding to the need, where is the doer? When, surrendering to the clear intelligence, the genuine humility, and the other divine qualities of your instructor, you drop your last limitations and merge into the sea of love that surrounds him, where is the devotee? Where is the teacher? Now then, if there is no ignorance, no delusion, no doer, no devotee, no instructor, who is walking on the gradual path? Who is mistaken? Who is claiming anything? Who is asking any questions?

Isn't it legitimate to use the term "enlightened person" when referring to someone from whom ignorance has been removed? If so, didn't this removal occur at some specific point in time?

Enlightenment is the absolute understanding that you are not a person. When this is understood, is there a person left from whom ignorance has been removed? Enlightenment is also the realization that time is an illusion. When this is realized, is there a specific point in time that can be assigned to this realization?

These answers may seem intellectual to you. However, I assure you that they are simply honest and straightforward, and that they take you directly to the truth. I am reluctant to use the term "enlightened person" because it implies the belief that a personal entity might ever reach enlightenment. When you think of a beautiful human being, one you may call "enlightened," his or her enlightenment originates from the absence of the idea of being anything objective. From the viewpoint of light, that is, in the absence of such a notion, nobody is enlightened, nobody is non-enlightened, everything is light. The direct path consists of taking this viewpoint and boldly staying there. In other words, understanding that you are not a limited entity, and feeling and living in accordance with this understanding. Although this position may seem unusual at first, you soon find that it is the door to the perfect way of living, just as a tennis player who has been taught the correct grip for the backhand realizes, after a series of strokes, that this new way of holding the racket creates the possibility for hitting the ball almost effortlessly, with increased power and precision.

လ

Although I know I am already that which I am seeking, thoughts still seem to prevent me from truly living in the present moment. How can I free myself from thinking?

There are three kinds of thoughts:

1. Practical thoughts, which are useful in conducting our business or our daily life. For instance, "I need to get some gas." These types of thoughts should not be suppressed. Once they have been given due consideration and the required steps have been taken, they leave us spontaneously.

2. Thoughts related to the ultimate, to our understanding of the non-dual perspective, such as, "I am already that for which I am looking." These thoughts come from the ultimate. If we welcome them, they purify the mind from its dualistic conditioning and eventually take us back to their source. They bring about clarity and foreshadow the bliss which is inherent to our real nature.

3. Thoughts related to the notion of being a personal entity, such as desires, fears, doubts, daydreaming, and other kinds of wishful thinking. Some thoughts of this third kind appear innocuous and are difficult to detect at first. A strong emotion that produces suffering and disharmony, such as jealousy or fear, can easily be detected. On the other hand, we may indulge pleasant thoughts for some time without noticing, such as imagining yourself vacationing on the beaches of the French Riviera.

It is a common error to consider any kind of thought as an obstacle to self-realization. Only the thoughts in the third category are obstacles to knowingly being the absolute. There are two ways to deal with these thoughts as they arise:

If we still believe that we are a limited personal entity and we notice such a thought, we should attempt to find its source, the ego. When we attempt to catch it, it vanishes and we experience our innate freedom for what seems to be a very brief moment. This glimpse of the truth reveals to us that we are not a personal entity. Repeated glimpses reinforce this revelation until it becomes a conviction.

Once we are convinced that we are not a personal entity, the thoughts of the third kind usually keep recurring for some time as a matter of habit, just as inertia keeps an electrical motor running after its power cord has been unplugged. In this case, there is no need to investigate the origin of these thoughts. We can simply drop them as soon as we notice them.

Sri Ramakrishna once said, "When an onion is completely peeled, all the layers are removed and no substance is left. Similarly, on analyzing the ego no entity can be found. Unfortunately, I still have a few layers to go!"

This last sentence is a typical thought of the third kind. Enjoy your thoughts about the ultimate and the peace that comes with them.

You indicated that daydreaming is always negative, because it takes one away from the present and into duality. However, it can also be creative, as evidenced by Kekule's realization of the structure of the benzene ring during a period of daydreaming.

This example is not one of daydreaming, but one of a meditative state in which the thinking process is totally free to evolve and explore all possibilities. We may experience this creative state during the transition between sleep and the waking state, a transitory moment when volition is usually weak. There are many examples of creative discoveries or inspirational moments of this kind in the arts and sciences. In this state, no notion of a personal entity is involved. We are the witness of a free thinking process which evolves through visualization and spatial representation. These thoughts become more and more subtle, until they finally dissolve in intelligence, being, and happiness. Coming out of this non-experience, the scientist or the philosopher says, "I understand," the artist is inspired to write a poem or a symphony, and the ordinary person finds the solution to a daily-life problem which was haunting him.

This meditative state may appear at first to be a dream state, because the objects that are present in consciousness at that time are of a subtle quality: they are mental images and thoughts, not external sense perceptions, as in the waking state. What makes this state a meditative state is the absence of a person. The subject *of* this state is not present *in* this state as a person acting, enjoying, and suffering. The subject is the pure witness. This state provides us with a natural entry point to meditation. When we wake up, this transitional state is often still present. Instead of letting the concerns relating to the objects of the waking state gradually take possession of our mind, we can allow the fragrance of the transitional state to permeate into the waking state. In other words, if we remain in the remembrance of the peace and freedom of deep sleep, for as long as this peace accepts us, it will become more and more clear that the waking state literally "wakes up in us," and that we don't wake up in it as previously believed. After a while, we will feel the continuous presence of that background of peace during our daily activities.

By contrast, daydreaming is a kind of mental activity through which the personal entity escapes an actual and current life situation which is "boring" or "painful," and projects itself into a subtle fantasy world. This type of thought usually goes unnoticed, because, unlike other forms of egoistic thoughts and emotions, such as anger, hatred, jealousy, envy, or greed, it doesn't appear to disrupt the social harmony or bring about any psychological suffering. After all, to take oneself for a person is well accepted and encouraged in our Western society, and daydreaming is considered to be innocuous. For these reasons, this activity is an ideal hiding place for the ego, and any serious truth-seeker should be aware of this problem.

When my mind becomes still during meditation, I am still aware of sense perceptions. How does this relate to the story about the arrow-maker whose attention was so perfect that he was not aware of the king's wedding procession passing by outside? Is my meditation incorrect?

There are two kinds of meditation: meditation with an object and non-objective (or non-dual) meditation.

The first kind of meditation requires focusing the attention onto a specific object, gross or subtle, such as a statue or a mental image of the divine, various bodily sensations, a series of sacred sounds, or a concept. In this process, an effort is necessary in order to remove one's attention from the usual objects of desire, which, if successful, gives the impression that the ego is weakened. The mind is focused on the object and one experiences a stillness, an absence of thoughts or emotions other than those referring to the object of meditation, even in the presence of the king going by in his wedding procession. However, the samadhi which is experienced is a mind-created state which has a beginning and an end. Sooner or later, the yogin must come out of samadhi. Unfortunately, the ego is still present, along with its cortege of fears, desires, and pains.

A special form of meditation with an object is one in which the object is a void or blank. In this process, one makes an effort to keep the mind free from thoughts or sensations. Sometimes a tool, such as the repetition of a sacred formula or some form of breath-control is used to achieve this end. As in any kind of meditation with an object, a temporary weakening of the ego ensues, and the mind may experience, for some time, a blank state, an absence of thoughts and sensations, or simply an absence of thoughts, depending on the depth and the nature of the experience. However, this is also a mind-created state which has a beginning and an end. This form of meditation is often mistakenly believed to be non-objective meditation. This is not the case because the absence of objects (sensations and thoughts) is still a very subtle projected object. Although this state may temporarily bring some satisfaction, and even unleash some mind powers, it turns out to be barren. The meditator remains within the prison of the mind, and the fullness of the heart remains unknown to him. This state is devoid of the absolute freedom, creative joyfulness, and wonderful immortality of the natural non-dual state.

31

In non-objective meditation, our attention is drawn toward the non-objective, the ultimate subject, consciousness. This occurs spontaneously as a result of understanding. At the first stage, the truth-seeker is asked to notice that the happiness for which he is really looking, the causeless bliss he experiences in the presence of his teacher, is non-objective, meaning "not contained in any object, gross or subtle." When this is understood, the mind, which can only grasp mentations (thoughts and sense perceptions), realizes that it can't have access to the non-objective realm; that any attempt to secure happiness through the mind is doomed to failure. As a result, the mind soon finds itself in a natural state of stillness. In this natural form of meditation, sensations or thoughts are neither sought nor avoided; they are simply welcomed and seen off. It could be described as a total openness, in which we are totally open to our sense perceptions, bodily sensations, emotions, feelings, and thoughts.

We could compare these mentations with the different characters of a play. As long as we find the play interesting, our attention is completely drawn by the actors in the foreground. But, if there is a weak moment, our attention progressively relaxes until we suddenly become aware of the background, of the stage. In the same way, as our attention relaxes and becomes global, unfocused, open, and disinterested (this detachment follows from our understanding that these mentations have really nothing to offer in terms of real happiness), we suddenly become aware of the background of consciousness, which is revealed as the ultimate immortality, splendor, and happiness we were seeking.

It isn't necessary for the actors to leave the stage in order for us to be aware of the background of the set. Similarly, the absence of mentations is not a prerequisite for recognition of our true self. However, when the actors leave and our attention relaxes, we have an opportunity to be aware of the background. In the same way, we have the opportunity to knowingly experience our real nature when a mentation merges with consciousness.

The attitude of welcoming, which is the essence of non-objective meditation, is easily and naturally conveyed to a sincere truth-seeker by "induction," in the presence of someone who has merged with the background.

ॐ

You imply that every gradual path is ego-driven. Should I stop meditating twice a day?

There is nothing wrong with two daily meditations. On the contrary, I recommend that you sit in stillness twice a day, preferably before going to sleep and right after waking up. Now, the question is, what does sitting in stillness mean? It means to sit free from dualizing thoughts, to sit in being; in non-doing, not in becoming, not in end-gaining. When the notion of a person arises, a person trying to achieve some goal, such as becoming the Prime Minister or a realized human being, simply be aware of it, take note of it. Don't try to eliminate it, don't judge yourself. It is simply a recurring habit which will lose its poisonous character if left alone. The moment it is noticed it becomes neutralized.

Be aware of fear, desire, and boredom as they arise. Don't try to escape. Welcome them and give them the opportunity to unfold in your loving presence. Notice that these feelings have thought-like and sensation-like components, related to the notion of being a person. The thought-like component can be swiftly dealt with by asking, "Who is afraid? Who is in a state of lack? Who is getting bored?" The bodily sensations should be given space and time to evolve, unfold, and tell their stories. Don't try to get rid of them or maintain them. Simply welcome them and see them off. In this way, your attention is removed from the objective realm and is spontaneously transferred to your real nature. It is the only way to facilitate this transfer, because the mind can't directly focus on that which is beyond the mind. Any attempt to do so would tie us to the subject-object realm and would, therefore, be doomed to failure.

৯৬

I am unable to realize the truth at the moment. This means that I am not realized.

There is only the truth. How could we possibly not see it, since there is only it? Whatever is known at the moment, in the timeless now, is the truth. The knower, the known, and knowing are one, and this oneness is the living truth. A second later, a new thought arises saying, "I just knew this or that" and this new thought demotes the non-dual truth to the rank of "this" or "that," an

33

object known by a limited subject, the personal entity. This new thought is also the truth. There is no thinker of this thought in the now. The thought, its thinker, and thinking are one, as always. We have never left the now. How could we?

Equally meaningless as the concept of a "realized person" is the concept of a "non-realized" person. If you think you are "non-realized," it implies that you don't know what realization is. If you don't know what realization is, how do you know that you aren't realized? You might discover that you have always been realized, and like a man married to two wives, one divine and immortal, the other human and perishable, you simultaneously live at two levels: the relative level of subject-object relations, and the absolute and timeless level of pure, non-dual consciousness. In the meantime, don't indulge in dualizing thoughts, such as "realized" and "non-realized." Get rid, once and for all, of these erroneous concepts which originate from the false notion that you are a personal entity, and don't allow them to resurface in the mind. This attitude could be called "living according to one's deep understanding."

What does the "direct path" you describe entail?

The direct path means direct understanding, and the boldness to act according to this understanding. You don't need to understand everything that is said here. Start with what you understand directly, not with what you merely believe. Start with what you feel in deep agreement with, and live accordingly.

Isn't deep sleep a return of my ego to the womb where it can hide from the realities of life?

Speaking about your ego in this way implies that you know your ego "which returns to the womb every night." You are implying that your ego is an object of which you are the witness or knower. Do you know the knower of your ego? Find out for yourself whether this knower ever returns to the womb to sleep, or whether this knower is the ever-present and eternally aware womb of all appearances and disappearances.

The stillness we occasionally experience between two mentations in the waking state is totally aware, whereas deep sleep seems (admittedly to the waking state) an absence of any such awareness. How could both experiences possibly be identical?

You acknowledge that you are speaking of deep sleep as it appears from the vantage point of the waking state. In other words, you are referring to the deep sleep state rather than to deep sleep as it is subjectively experienced. From your vantage point, your remark is true. The subjective stillness between two mentations, which the Indian tradition calls Turiya, the ultimate reality, is alive and aware, whereas the deep sleep state, construed to be pure blank, or nothingness, is dead and unconscious. However, so is the stillness between mentations, when seen from the vantage point of the mind as a blank state or an objective nothingness. Having had a glimpse of the awareness and liveliness of the interval between mentations, we are open to the awareness and liveliness of deep sleep, which is also an interval between two mentations.

The ego is not present in this stillness and has no desire for it. It wants to maintain its existence through the dynamism of the mind. When this dynamism stops, the truth is revealed in the absence of the ego. The ego's uselessness becomes manifest, just as the temporary absence of an incompetent, lazy, and nasty employee allows his manager to realize that the business can be run more efficiently without him. For this reason, it isn't the ego who desires deep sleep, in which it is absent. The invitation comes from the absolute.

A purification is accomplished spontaneously if we welcome our thoughts and bodily sensations during the transition between the waking state and deep sleep. Our concerns leave the mind, one by one, and the traces of the struggles of the day that is ending leave the body, one by one, until the entire body-mind structure becomes a single fullness of light, awareness, and timeless presence.

This could be called "entering deep sleep knowingly." The key is to do this welcoming meditation every night before falling asleep. During these moments you let everything that is not you depart, so that you can enter the sanctuary of the night with the nakedness, the humility, and the innocence of a newborn child.

3

Love Never Dies

People who pause and honestly ask themselves, "Who or what am I?" will quickly admit that they don't know. What is our real nature?

I am not sure they should quickly admit that they don't know, because a thorough investigation is needed to bring about the maturity of a deep experience. If, after trying to understand who you are, the answer is, "I don't know," I would say, "That is fine. Look again." This inquiry about who we are is a serious undertaking. It has to become the only question in our life, not just a question we repeat verbally: "Who am I? Who am I? Who am I?" It has to come unexpectedly, when a task has been accomplished, when we are in a moment of openness.

This question may appear in various forms, such as: "What is life?", "What is happiness?", "What is truth?" All of these questions are equivalent. They boil down to the single question, "Who am I?" When one of these questions spontaneously arises, we should respond by opening our heart, giving it all the attention and love of which we are capable, and by living with it. Then the quest remains alive in us. It opens up a path of understanding and clarifies the mind. We find ourselves in openness, open to the unknown, and in this quietness there is the opportunity to be taken beyond, to the understanding that we are that which we are seeking.

You pointed out that it isn't wise to deal with the question, "Who am I?" too quickly. There are people who devote their lives to this question, or to a particular facet of it. For example, a philosopher may dedicate his life to answering the question, "What is life?" while the physicist may devote himself to understanding, "What is the world?" and the psychologist may spend his life with, "What is a person?" Are any of these approaches, carried to their natural end, possible routes to our real nature?

These ways of research don't bring the seeker anywhere. At best, they bring him to the understanding that he was traveling down a dead-end street. This is already an achievement. The real question, "Who am I?" requires a great deal of maturity, otherwise the search is not genuine, because it is corrupted by the desires and the misconceptions of the ego. I may be a professional writer inquiring about my real nature, but if my investigation is corrupted by the desire to sell my books or win a Nobel Prize, then I am not looking for truth, but for money and fame.

Maturity comes when the seeker, in all earnestness, in all honesty, in all genuineness, arrives at an absolute, "I don't know." When this level of maturity is reached, he will meet a teacher who will help him on his way to the ultimate answer. He may find his teacher at an earlier stage, but this level of maturity will, so to speak, compel the encounter with a teacher. The presence of the teacher enables the seeker to break the vicious circle in which he is trapped due to the mind being unable to reach beyond itself. In the living presence of the teacher, out of an impalpable experience, out of a non-event, higher intelligence is born.

Is a meeting with a teacher necessary in order to understand the truth?

I assume that by "meeting with a teacher," you mean a meeting with a living teacher.

Yes, on the phenomenal plane.

In principle, no, but for all practical purposes, yes. In principle, no, since the teacher is not a person. The teacher is the ultimate reality, not a body or a mind. In practice, yes, because the seeker can't extricate himself from the vicious circle of the ego. The ego can't kill itself. Even if an individual has a premonition of the truth and becomes an earnest seeker, when dissatisfaction about the usual objects of desire steps in, a living contact with what we could call a personification of the truth is still needed.

During this contact, the teacher brings the student to a state of not knowing, in which the mind gives up the search. Only in this total openness can the real teaching begin, and the beginning of the real teaching, in the silence of the heart, is also its end.

ॐ

How can we live in harmony with others?

A person can never live in harmony with other persons. He can only live in harmony with others when there are no others.

Why does love between human beings seem so fragile?

When a man and woman meet (this kind of love seems to be more fragile than love between parents and children) there is a polarity between them. There is a sexual polarity coming from the male and female elements in them, and there is also a more general gender polarity that exists between men and women. Out of this polarity, an attraction is born, which has a biological mission to accomplish: the perpetuation of the human race.

There is nothing wrong with this instinct. It has its own beauty and brings about enjoyment. But real love lies beyond. If there is no meeting in real love, the attraction eventually fades away, in the same way that a battery gets discharged when we connect its two poles. The conflicting desires and fears of both partners, which up until now were hidden by the cloud of their mutual attraction, reappear, and the relationship comes to an end.

In this case there wasn't a real relationship in the first place. The love was fragile because the relationship was not grounded in real love. If there is a deeper meeting of the hearts, or rather a meeting in the heart, this love is beyond time and space. It can never disappear.

The saying, "Love never dies" comes from this intuition. Real love stays with us forever. It isn't stored in memory. It is a kind of remembrance that comes from the core of our being. When we remember a loved one, we may at first see his face, hear his voice, but these objective elements soon disappear in real love, our common ground, awareness.

෨

Is sexual pleasure ever morally wrong?

Sexual pleasure *per se* is neither morally wrong nor morally right. It all depends on the purity of the heart. Purity of the heart means love. Love makes everything sacred. Real love is not a relationship between male and female, not even a companionship between man and woman. It goes much deeper. It is the friendliness in which two apparently separate human beings melt together. If a relationship is grounded in real love, sexuality is an offering, a celebration of life. It becomes sacred. In the absence of real love, it is only a function of the body.

But, whether functioning well or not, sexual behavior simply does not fall within the moral domain?

From this perspective, there is no such thing as codified morality. If there is love between two men or between two women, for instance, and if sexuality becomes a way of expressing this love, it is sacred. Love doesn't exclude anything. Love is all-welcoming, all-encompassing, open to anyone who is open to it.

෨

Is it possible to have a relationship in which the ego is not involved?

Yes, of course. I would even say that it is the only way to have a real relationship, because relationship means relation, contact. If I take myself for a person, then there is another, and there is a relation between an object and another object, which means no relation at all, since two objects can never contact one another.

Why is that?

Real contact is in the heart. Objects, as such, have no heart. Real relationship is in the heart, in oneness. There are circumstances in which you can feel this beauty. One day, I was waiting for a friend at the airport. He was seated at the rear of the plane, so I had an opportunity to see the other incoming passengers, and their relatives waiting for them at the gate. I vividly remember the joy of a family being reunited, the tears in their eyes, their spontaneous and affectionate gestures, their smiling faces. So, of course, there are real relationships.

Are you saying that they weren't people in that moment? They weren't persons?

Absolutely. I could feel their joy in me. I was there unnoticed, but one with them, with the beauty of the scene.

ॐ

What is sin?

Sin is nonsense. There is no sin, because there is no sinner in the first place. The only sin is to take oneself for a sinner. I grant that there may be inadequate behavior, an action that originates from a fragmented view of the situation. Such an action will haunt one until the situation is seen again in its totality, at which point the underlying conflict finds its resolution in intelligence. But, there is no need to willfully recollect these "sins." Such a recollection only strengthens the ego. There is no point in condemning oneself as a sinner or in trying to change oneself. Sense of guilt and desire to change also reinforce the ego. One only need see these so-called sins for what they are, not take oneself for their doer, and forget them.

Sin is a "big deal" in Christian societies like ours, and there is a widespread feeling, if not fear, that to take such a position, to simply forget our wrongdoings as we go along, might allow further wrongdoings that could have been avoided, had we taken a look at what we were doing. If we don't examine our mistakes, there may be a tendency to continue to commit them.

I am not advising you to ignore faulty behavior and not try to understand it. On the contrary, I say yes, understand, but don't attribute the action to yourself. Don't take yourself for a sinner. Understand that you were the witness of the deed, not its doer, and forget it.

Are you saying all mistakes can be traced back to the ego, and that the ego is the original mistake, a case of mistaken identity?

This is certainly true for all ethical mistakes. If I am learning how to drive, I am going to make mistakes, and these mistakes are all right. They are part of the learning process. They won't haunt me in the future. However, if I behave badly toward somebody, my wrongdoing will haunt me, and I will come to the understanding that I have to undo the mischief. In this case, I should immediately do my best to remedy the situation, if possible, and then forget it. But, there is no sinner, there is nobody who needs to be forgiven.

ॐ

42

How can people learn to live without fear?

They should learn to live with their fear. If they try to get rid of fear, they will be caught in a vicious circle, because fear originates from the ego, from the idea of being a separate entity, and this same ego, looking for pleasurable situations and avoiding the unpleasant ones, wants to get rid of fear.

Please explain how fear arises from the ego as a separate entity. Most people's experience is that fear arises from threatening situations, from possible physical danger, for example, and that it happens to, rather than comes from, the ego.

There are two kinds of fear. There is a fear coming from the instinct of survival, common to men and animals. This fear is perfectly natural, there is nothing wrong with the body preparing itself to face a threatening situation.

So the notion of living free from fear does not exclude experiencing fear when biological survival is in question?

No. That is a very deep conditioning that belongs to the body.

And it doesn't cause problems . . .

It doesn't cause problems if there is no identification with the body, because then it is seen like a cloud appearing and dissolving in the sky. It may even be useful.

If somebody doesn't take himself for a person, are you saying that fear will arise, be seen simply like an object appearing in the body, and the person will act in the most appropriate way?

Yes. If you are under attack, this fear may trigger in your body the right supplement of adrenaline you need to run faster than your assailant.

43

Right!

However, psychological fear is of a different nature. You may remember situations when, as a child, you imagined monsters, and, although they were your own creations, there was a point when they took on a life of their own, bringing about real fear in you. These psychological creations trigger the same biological mechanisms of fear with adrenaline secretion, but their origin is now completely different: it is a thought created by the person.

In this case, what is threatened is the ego; its survival is in question.

Yes, psychological fear comes from the ego. If I think and feel that I am a personal entity, then everything that is not "I" is a potential threat to me. If I am everything, if there is nothing other than "I," of what could I be afraid? The real source of psychological fear is the ego. The question was, "How can people learn to live without fear?" Let's first understand the uselessness of trying to get rid of any specific fear. Assume I am afraid of ghosts, and that makes me frightened and depressed. I undergo a ten-year psychoanalysis, until I have the insight of some event in my early childhood being the underlying cause of my fear of ghosts. That ends the analysis. I am declared cured of my fear of ghosts, and indeed I am. Three months thereafter, I again fall into a serious depression. This time, I am no longer afraid of ghosts; I am afraid of becoming ill and dying.

Are you suggesting that the fear of ghosts was never your real fear, that all along it was the fear of dying?

I am suggesting that the ghosts were a superimposition onto an underlying fear. If a manipulation at the level of the mind removes this superimposition, its root cause has not been eliminated, and a new superimposition will soon come up.

Are you saying that it isn't possible to live as a person without fear?

Exactly.

Because there is always fear of death . . .

Because fear is the person, and the person is fear. Fear and desire are the same thing. Fear is a negative form of desire. Fear is, "I don't want this to happen" which is the same as, "I hope this won't happen." Desire or fear is the substance of the ego. The ego as such, as the pure thought "I am," can't last long. This thought, "I am," soon dies in the non-experience of being, in its source, awareness. The mechanism of fear and desire has to come in to lend some appearance of continuity to the ego. Until I have avoided the dreadful event or obtained the desired object, the ego lives. Therefore, the only radical cure for fear, which is also a cure for desire, is the understanding that we are not this ego, subject to fear and desire.

This understanding comes as a result of a deep inquiry. To understand this at the conceptual level is important, but this understanding has to go much deeper, because fear and desire have a profound impact on the texture and structure of the body. When we feel fear, we must face it in order to understand it deeply. We have to see its source, the notion of being a personal entity, but we also have to welcome it as a bodily sensation, as a perception. We should not be afraid of our fear. We should let it appear in us and see it for what it is, a set of bodily sensations.

ॐ

After encountering this perspective, I feel that every notion I have of myself and of the world is wrong, and I have no idea where to start in order to put things right. Can you suggest a starting point?

The encounter with this perspective was the starting point. To question all the previous notions and to arrive at the feeling, "I don't know" is a very good sign. This perspective does not replace false notions with new ones. It simply enables you to see the concepts you had for what they were: illusions, mere thought forms having no real connection with one another. This is enough. So, live in your innocence, live with your "I don't know." Don't assert anything. Don't reach any final conclusion. Don't judge. Be open, learn, and understand. Know and enjoy what you are from moment to moment.

45

How can I move from there toward some kind of clarification? How can I live from moment to moment, simply being open, and enjoy it? Do you have a practical suggestion?

I would say, "Live with the desire for truth. Let it be your guide." The desire for truth comes from truth itself. It brings about higher intelligence that will, in time, clarify all questions. Enjoy the path, since there is already a joyful component in understanding. Don't take yourself for a limited entity now that you have seen, at least in a glimpse, that you are awareness beyond mentations. Keep this understanding as a treasure. Go back to it when it invites you. Live with it and let it do the work.

How would you compare the difference between the views of the world held by Western science and non-dualism? Are there any fundamental similarities, or are they radically different?

They are radically different. These perspectives exclude one another. From the point of view of Western science, of physics, there is an objective world "out there" existing independently of awareness, and this alleged world (as the non-dualist would say) is the subject matter of science. The scientist starts with the study of a world the existence of which he has no proof, whereas the non-dualist, taking a radically different approach, commences from the only certainty he has, the only certainty we can have, that of being. This certainty can never be denied. It is our moment-to-moment experience. For this reason, unlike the scientist, the non-dualist takes a firm stand in certainty and in reality.

I am not ignoring the changes in modern physics that originate from the theory of relativity and from quantum mechanics. These changes lead us to question the validity of the materialistic view of an independent universe comprised of solid particles. At the extra-galactic and at the subatomic scales the universe is no longer what it appeared to be at the human scale. Notions we held to be absolute truth, such as absolute space, absolute time, causality, locality, and determinism turn out to have only a relative validity. The ancient epistemological framework, atomistic materialism and strict realism, seems to be inconsistent with modern physics as demonstrated by Pr. d'Espagnat. The non-dualist perspective might, perhaps, offer a more satisfactory epistemological foundation to modern science. However, future discoveries in science will never be able to prove

46

or disprove its validity. The immediate experience of awareness remains forever outside the field of science, a domain limited by design to objective facts and relative truths. Non-dualism has little to contribute to science. At the most, it is possible that intuitions originating from a non-fragmented view of the world might lead to new formulations or discoveries in the field of science.

Scientific breakthroughs of the twentieth century may also have a liberating effect. By questioning the world as existing independently from consciousness, they pave the way toward the ultimate understanding. They open the truth seeker to the possibility that the world might be a phenomenon that appears in, exists in, and disappears into universal consciousness. Seekers cease then to be physicists. They become philosophers, metaphysicists, poets. They cross this philosophical Rubicon when, going beyond the phenomenal order, they include within the scope of their investigation the noumenon, consciousness.

So, the difference between these two perspectives derives from their different points of departure. The point of departure of the non-dualist is the certainty of "I am," whereas the scientist's certainty of the existence of the external world is supported by the common experience of virtually the whole of humanity. It is a collective view, not an individual view, as is the non-dualist's. Would that be correct?

Yes. Once you grant existence to the so-called objective world, existing independently of awareness, then you grant existence to the whole of humanity. From the vantage point of the non-dualist, the undeniable subject is the subject matter. From the point of view of the scientist, the alleged object is the subject matter.

Are you saying the non-dualist takes himself to be the only subject, and that the existence of the whole of humanity, along with the rest of the objective world is in question?

It depends on what you call "himself." What the non-dualist calls "myself" or "I" is not limited to a specific body, to a specific mind. Body and mind are limitations that are superimposed onto awareness. The non-dualist starts from experience. The scientist, although he claims to start from experience, starts, in fact, from a concept: the existence of an alleged world. He then thoroughly studies this alleged world.

Could you clarify what you mean by the word "experience" when you say that the non-dualist starts from experience, whereas the scientist starts from a concept, rather than from experience? Is the ordinary experience of the average person no more than concepts?

The essence of our being is not a concept.

For each of us?

Of course. It is life itself. It is beyond any concept. Concepts are superimpositions, such as: I am a man, I am forty years old, I am a physician. All these distinctive features are mere superimpositions onto our real nature. The substratum, which is free from limitations, doesn't have any boundaries, doesn't need a knower to reveal itself, and is self-evident and autonomous.

I am struck by your statement that, while each of us is life itself, the non-dualist doesn't grant existence to the rest of humanity, in the objective world, in the way the scientist does. He puts everything in question, including the rest of humanity. Isn't there a contradiction in that?

When we say that the non-dualist sees humanity as non-real, we mean that he doesn't see it as an object, as something that is separate from awareness, from himself. He sees, instead, humanity as one with himself. From this vision of oneness, of non-separateness, real compassion, ethical behavior, and justice follow. We should not consider the sage as some crazy solipsist, isolated in his ivory tower, denying existence to the rest of mankind and granting existence only to himself as a person. On the contrary, the truth-lover starts by questioning his own existence as a person, as a separate entity, asking, "Who am I? Am I this body? Am I this mind? Am I this limited entity?" He isn't interested in theories, but in reality. He starts with the only field of experience that is available to him, that is, himself.

The answer to this question can never be a positive statement. It is the understanding of what we are not. When what we are not is eliminated, not by effort or by violence, but as a result of understanding, what remains is our real nature. It is an experience, but not an experience in time and space, and for this reason we could call it a non-experience, a non-event. In this non-event, we are one with mankind. It is a non-excluding, an all-comprehending perspective.

So the non-dualist does disagree with positing the existence of the rest of humanity as a group of separate conscious entities which could agree or disagree with him. He, rather, leaves open the possibility that the whole of humanity is one with him . . .

The non-dualist isn't interested in concepts. He is only interested in his true nature. After seeing his misconceptions for what they are, what remains is a non-state, a non-event devoid of fear and desire, in which certainty and peace prevail. Because he starts from reality, he soon reaches his goal, reality. Reality reaches reality. Unity reaches unity. Because the scientist starts from a mere hypothesis, a misconception, his point of arrival is as shaky and unstable as his point of departure. He can never reach a completely satisfactory understanding. He is bound to be eternally dissatisfied, moving from object to object in an endless process.

The non-dual perspective is certainly radical and intriguing. How can I know that this isn't just another sophisticated form of conditioning, much like others, however radically different it might appear at first sight?

You can reach a completely satisfactory answer to your question because the answer lies within you, or more precisely, the answer is you. Any other approach requires beginning with a certain degree of belief. Belief belongs to memory, to the mind, to the past. Belief can never be a solid foundation, since it is a concept you take for granted without understanding.

In this perspective, we take nothing for granted, radically nothing. We could say that it is the ultimate scientific vantage point, with the difference that the subject matter in this case is not, as we have seen, an object, since we don't even assume the existence of objects. Because we make no assumptions, the understanding we arrive at is free from the past, from conditioning. The mind, having completed its investigation, becomes still, and in this stillness our desire for truth finds its ultimate fulfillment.

This fulfillment is analogous to the satisfaction we experience when, after having thought about a problem, the solution suddenly comes to us unexpectedly, from our true nature, which is intelligence itself. In a way, the solution finds itself in us. We call that process understanding. However, in this case, since our comprehension relates to objects, this satisfaction is limited. Soon, we are again in a state of dissatisfaction. However, when this understanding, instead of bringing closure to a relative question, refers to the ultimate question, to the source of all questions, to the eternal subject, fulfillment is total.

4

Our True Nature Is Not an Object

What is our true nature?

It is not an object. It isn't something that can be perceived by the five senses or that can be conceived through the mind. Our false nature is always some kind of object. The body, for example, is an object. It is a collection of perceptions, sensations, and concepts of what our body is. The mind is also an object. However, our true nature is not an object.

It is very difficult to speak about it because words and the structure of language are designed to refer to objects. We have no words to speak about something which is non-objective. We have to use metaphors or negations to that effect. So, we say that we are not our body, we are not our mind. Nevertheless, *we are*. Our existence is something of which we all are absolutely certain. Everything else could be a mirage, an illusion, a dream. Even if this were the case, we still would have no doubt that *we are*.

Our true nature is elusive. We can't see it, touch it, conceive of it, or grasp it. On the other hand, it is the only thing the existence of which we can be sure. Thinking about it in this way, saying what it is not, unknowingly orients us toward our timeless background. We become available to it. That is all we can do, be open to it. We can't make it reveal itself. It reveals itself at its own pleasure as truth, beauty, love, and immortality.

51

Do you mean that it isn't revealed in some situations, such as non-beautiful ones? Why doesn't it reveal itself all the time?

Maybe it does reveal itself all the time and we are just looking the other way. Quite often the best place to hide an object is to put it in full sight. Our real self, so close and so luminous that it can't be seen with the eyes, has its hiding place in the immediacy of the now.

We would like to see it all the time, as an object in front of us, but that isn't possible, because objects come and go, are born and die. Its beauty lies in its not being an object. If it were an object we could and would lose it. Since it is what we are, we can't lose it. What prevents us from seeing it, from being it knowingly, is our desire to see it as an object. This attitude is what we may call "looking in the wrong direction." So the question is, what is the right direction? Even if we try to look toward the non-objective direction, we have to face the fact that the absence of any object is another kind of object. So, we have to go beyond the absence of objects. We have to reach the absence of their absence, which reveals itself as our all-pervading, all-encompassing presence.

At first, we try to look at our real nature as if it were an object. Then we understand that this attempt is doomed to failure. Next, we look at it as an absence of object, and at some point we understand that this search, too, is doomed to failure. Finally, we find ourself in a state of not knowing, a state in which the mind has exhausted all of its possibilities and has no further place to go. We reach the understanding that the mind cannot grasp this luminous awareness which enlightens it, and we become still. We have to make acquaintance with this not knowing, to get used to this new dimension, to discover that it is not nothingness. This silent presence is not a mere absence of thoughts. It is alive. It is life itself.

When I am in my garden I sometimes seem to experience what you were saying. Can this experience ever be conveyed through words?

It isn't a concept, so it can't be communicated as a concept, merely through words. I could communicate the concept of a differential equation through words, but we have to understand that our true nature is not a concept. Words can be used in two different ways. One way they can be used is to appeal to the logical, rational side of the mind. But, used in this way, all they can really do is to lead the mind to the understanding that our true nature is not a concept, and that the mind can't reach it by its own effort. When we understand fully that this dynamic process is doomed to failure, that it can't bring the happiness we are seeking, the mind becomes quiet. In the beginning, there may be some residual momentum in the thinking process, just as a motor keeps running for a while after its cord has been unplugged, but we are no longer a player in this game. This insight releases the energies that were used in trying to achieve happiness and allows them to flow back to their source.

There is another way in which words can be used. My answer to you isn't coming from memory, but from the now. It has within it certain ingredients which are the signature of its origin. If you listen to these words with a child-like innocence, they may resonate in you, and you may find yourself to be a welcoming presence. For that to happen, you have to be totally open. You have to set aside everything you have learned and everything you know, because the truth is always new and always appears unexpectedly. You have to be open multi-dimensionally, not just at the level of the intellect but also at the level of feelings and sensations. If you cannot, if thoughts or bodily sensations interfere with this openness, all you can do is take note of this interference. If you notice that you aren't listening, you already are listening. If you notice that you aren't welcoming, you already are welcoming. If you receive my words with the proper attitude, they will find the way to your heart.

How do you distinguish what you are talking about from meditation? Or are you talking about meditation?

I don't know what you mean by meditation. Tell me, because it is a word that has so many meanings.

Sitting in silence with your mantra or your breath, so that your mind is quieted and you are open to whatever is coming in.

In some forms of meditation the mind is focused on an object. It can be a mantra, the breath, the flame of a candle, an idol, a sacred scripture, or an image of a deity with all its divine qualities. The intent in this case is to eliminate what is not the object of the meditation in order to find a rest in the object. At some point, there is an immersion in the object of meditation through elimination of what is not meditated upon. This union is called samadhi. The rejection of what is not the object of meditation creates an

53

imbalance, so that the state reached as a result of this effort, however blissful or happy it may be, can't be maintained. If you take a closer look at this bliss, it is, for all practical purposes, not really different from any other object-generated happiness, such as the happiness you experience when you get a long-desired-for red Ferrari. It has a beginning in time and an end in time. The earnest truth-seeker soon finds that such a time-bound episode of happiness leaves him dissatisfied. He is looking for that which is timeless and discovers that the samadhi which can be reached as a result of objective meditation is finally the same kind of happiness he thought he was immunized against. Once this is understood the door is opened to real meditation.

Real meditation is spontaneous. It is pure welcoming, because there is no choosing of whatever appears in the field of consciousness. There is no selection. There is only choiceless allowing, be it of external perceptions, feelings, bodily sensations, thoughts, or their absence. Everything is equally allowed to come into existence, not as a practice, but because the mind has understood its own limitations. That is all the truth-seeker needs to do. No further spiritual practice needs to be undertaken.

In this openness we live in the now. There is nothing to gain, nothing to lose. Awareness is not something to be acquired at the end of a process. We already have all we need. We are fully equipped, without any missing parts. In the beginning, we may experience this total absence of problems, which has now become our new condition, as a neutral state. This is because the mind is still running like a motor whose cord has just been unplugged. When we become a little more acquainted with our new perspective, we feel the bliss of the now, which is causeless and absolutely non-objective. It is like tuning in to a new frequency and listening to a Mozart piano concerto after hearing several hours of garbage on the radio. Then we simultaneously live at two levels: the usual objective world in front, and a new level in the background from which the music, the beauty originates. This level is not a specifically localized place. It is a metaphysical space, the background of the mind, the core of our being.

When we live in listening, we will notice a change in our feelings, thoughts, the way we sense our body, and the way we interact with others. Welcoming is a universal law. The night is welcoming, the sky is welcoming, the birds and the trees are welcoming. When we are surrounded by welcoming human companions, we live in beauty. Our shared presence gives us a taste of what the lost paradise might have felt like.

5

Real Life Has No Purpose

Does life have a purpose?

Real life has no purpose. Real life is pure joy, pure freedom. Now, if by life you mean this existence between birth and death, it could be said that its purpose is to know the truth.

Some people feel that the purpose of this existence is to contribute to the greater good, help other people, do the best they can in their circumstances, and help their family. When you say that the goal is the single one of knowing the truth, how would you explain to them that this goal is more important than the ones toward which they are working?

First, there is no incompatibility between knowing the truth and being a good husband or wife, a good father or mother, a good citizen. On the contrary, only in the absence of the belief that we are a separate entity, an ego, a person, can we be open to real love, to real beauty, and live a happy, creative, and harmonious life.

If someone wants to pursue the truth while raising a family, earning a living, and dealing with his own private unhappiness, how is he to do this?

Through intelligence. Understanding doesn't require any material change in our way of living. We start with what is at hand, with an interrogation about who we are, our perceptions, feelings, and thoughts. This investigation into our own reality is not merely conceptual, but includes all aspects of our life.

Can such a pursuit be carried on in the midst of a hectic life?

Certainly, and it is the only way you can be sure that your happiness belongs to you, is your own treasure, that it doesn't depend on any external circumstances. If your happiness depends on external factors, such as harmonious surroundings, then your beautiful experience vanishes when you are at the post office, or when there is noise outside. So this experience was not really your own happiness, it was merely a happy state.

I understand that happiness itself can't depend on anything external . . .

A great maturity is already required to reach this understanding, because most people think that happiness lies in some kind of object.

Does one require circumstances in his life that are conducive to such an investigation, or can it be carried out in the midst of a busy professional and family life?

No change is required. The only requirement is to be totally open to situations, to face them without any prejudgment, without any intervention of personal memory, because they are always new. If we face a situation without any intention, free from fear and desire, this openness paves the way for an intuition that will lead to a decision or an action in total harmony with that situation. Such a decision may bring about an apparent change, but this change is not an escape from or an avoidance of the situation, because it doesn't originate from the person. It emanates from intelligence.

When you say that a person should face the situation without memory or intention, this isn't how people usually enter into business or social situations. They are there for a purpose, with an intention. They enter into the situation remembering whatever is necessary to carry out their intentions. Why should they change their approach to their everyday situations, given that some kind of memory and some sort of intention will certainly play a role?

Some "know-how" is necessary to carry out professional tasks or daily life activities. For instance, as a physician, you have acquired knowledge and skills that belong to your profession. When required in a given situation, in the presence of a patient, this knowledge comes back to you effortlessly. There is absolutely nothing wrong with such functional concepts or actions that apparently arise from memory.

But, if I go about my daily work struggling, full of fear and desire, I have to ask myself, "What are my motivations? Who am I doing that for? What is my ultimate goal?"

We often assign ourselves goals in life (sometimes our parents and teachers have preassigned these goals), and never question them again. We go on with our life, totally programmed, totally conditioned. It would be wise to pause, and find out what we really want, what we really need.

Are you suggesting that there should be no psychological memory, and no psychological intent, when a person enters a business situation or a social situation, but that practical, functional memories that arise from the situation are perfectly fine?

Yes. I am amazed by the amount of energy executives and professionals in the business community devote to struggling with themselves, and against each other, in order to achieve personal goals. Most of their energy is spent in this fruitless struggle, and only a small part of it is left for the efficient fulfillment of their duties. This constant state of conflict generates suffering both in them and in the people around them. Why does this happen? How can we stop this war?

We first have to see the situation, because when we see it, maturity and intelligence come in. When we inquire deeply into this conflict, we discover that it originates from the ego, and that all this mess has a single purpose: the survival and happiness of the individual entity we believe we are.

So, to pursue life's main purpose, the truth, and to do it with less suffering, we should continue to enter into everyday situations, but less personally or even not personally, not as a person.

Yes. We should develop a new way of approaching the situations, an impersonal way. If we try to escape from a situation by avoiding it, we will have to confront it again, sooner or later. Therefore, it is absurd to postpone facing it. We have to deal with the facts as they appear, but not from the vantage point of a personal entity. We should face them from a more "scientific" or experimental perspective: without prejudging, without projecting any conclusion, simply seeing the components of the situation as they actually are. We should let the facts tell the story. When the situation is allowed to unfold, then, at some point, clarity appears and the action or the non-action that comes out of this clarity doesn't leave any traces behind.

ॐ

You say that this world is an illusion. How did you discover that?

The question behind this question is, "You say that this world is an illusion. How can I discover that?"

Absolutely!

When I say that this world is an illusion, I don't mean that this world doesn't exist. I simply mean that this world doesn't exist as an object that is separate or distinct from awareness. In other words, this world is not autonomous as classical physics would like us to believe. It can't be denied when perceived, as a perception, but can't be proven to exist when not perceived.

But, will you agree that an illusion exists as what it is, namely an illusion, an appearance?

Yes. An illusion is comprised of two elements: an underlying reality and a superimposed illusory concept. When you see a rope in the dark, you may mistakenly take it for a snake. But, when you turn on the light, you see that the only reality of the snake was the rope. There was never a snake in the first place. The snake was a complete illusion. An illusion is nonexistent. The snake never existed. The reality of the snake was the rope.

This is difficult to grasp because, although you are saying the snake never existed, I may not only have seen the snake, I may be able to tell you what color it was, how long it was, and so on. So, it can't be said that there was absolutely nothing. Furthermore, I didn't see the rope.

Of course. The color and all the other characteristics of the snake were a bunch of concepts bundled together to form the illusion. However, your claim that you didn't see the rope is false. You saw nothing but the rope. You simply didn't recognize it for what it really was, and superimposed the notion of a snake onto it. In the same way, the notion that there is a world out there, separate from us, is an illusion. What we perceive is reality itself. Most people don't recognize it for what it is, and superimpose onto it the notion of an external and independent world.

The world is in the position of the snake. It seems to be there, but is not.

Exactly. It is an alleged world. Now, what is in the position of the rope? Before the presence of the snake, after the presence of the snake, and during the presence of the snake, in reality, there is the rope. Before the presence of the world, after the presence of the world, and during the presence of the world, there is awareness. Thus, the only reality is awareness.

You said, on another occasion, that there is a continuous background of awareness both behind and between mentations. Why is that important, and how can I know that it is so for sure? How can I be certain, based on my own experience, that this is actually so?

The mind is made out of thoughts and perceptions, what we could call mentations. Nobody would challenge the fact that there is awareness during the presence of a mentation.

No.

So your question is, "How can I be aware of the fact that there is awareness between two mentations?" The mentations are the mind. This interval between two mentations doesn't belong to the objective mind. It is beyond the mind, totally out of reach. We can't perceive it through our five senses, we can't conceptualize it.

How is it that we are here discussing it, if we can't think it or conceive it? We seem to be talking about it.

What we can conceive is the fact that it is inconceivable. Conceiving that it is inconceivable brings about a purification of the mind. As a consequence of this understanding, our mind leaves the old patterns, the old belief that what we are is something that can be conceived or perceived as an object, such as a mind or a body. When the mind comes to the understanding that it has no access to this awareness which is present during and between mentations, it becomes quiet. But, the conviction that there is consciousness between two mentations never comes from the mind, from logical reasoning. It can only come from the experience of reality. When we ask ourselves, "Who am I?" and understand deeply that what we are is not perceivable and not conceivable, we remain as awareness. It is not a verbal answer, not a concept, not a perception. It is a living answer that brings with it its own conviction, its own certainty.

We can also experience it at the end of a thought that refers to our true nature. Such a thought is not centrifugal; it has no other place to go than to the inwardness of the heart. And when the thought about our intimate reality dies in its source, there is a moment of grace. In a single experience, beyond time, we are splendor, eternity, and love.

I love my desires. They make me feel alive. I don't see why I should renounce them.

Love your desires. Don't try to fight them. Welcome them. If you struggle against them, there is no way open for you to understand their origin. Intelligence starts with love. Love your desires, and understand what your deepest desire is. Whenever you find yourself desiring an object, ask yourself, "Will this object bring me the happiness I really want?" If the answer is, "Yes" then go ahead and learn from the experience. By loving your desires, by inquiring about them, you will come to understand that they all are superimposed onto the desire for peace and happiness, the desire to find your own nature, your real home.

If we welcome our desires, and even love them, aren't we actually indulging them? Is your suggestion that we welcome our desires any different from indulging them?

Yes. You can indulge in desires only if you think that the acquisition of the desired object will bring about the kind of happiness for which you are really looking. Once you have been informed, once you have acknowledged for yourself that the happiness you are seeking is not and can never be produced by any object, you are open to a new dimension. Then a detachment is born in you that is a spontaneous by-product of this understanding. This detachment allows you to maintain some distance between you, as awareness, and the emerging desire in you. You are no longer "stuck" to the desire. There is some space, some room for change, understanding, and learning.

ॐ

We assume that we are the dreamer that appears in our dreams at night. You say this is not so. Why?

When we wake up, we know for sure that we aren't the elephant we dreamt we were. There is no doubt that the world we were dreaming was a mere illusion, and by the same token, the personality we assumed in the dream was itself part of the dream, and so, an illusion. In the dream we may have a different gender, a different shape; we may be a bird or an elephant.

63

That is true, but in the way you are speaking of it, "In the dream . . . we may be a bird, or an elephant," there is the notion that we are doing the dreaming.

The so-called dreaming state and the so-called waking state share a common background. When there is a dream, this common background, the dreamer, and the dreamed are one; there is only dreaming.

Yes.

Dreaming and awareness are one.

Dreaming is a form of awareness?

Dreaming is awareness.

It is awareness of dream objects.

When there is dreaming, there is only dreaming. There is no object dreamed. The substance of the dream is actually nothing other than awareness. That is why I say dreaming is awareness. Similarly, when there is waking, waking is awareness. So, awareness is the common background that is present during waking, dreaming, deep sleep, and, also, between these states.

So, the felt continuity between the dreamer and the dream ego, the notion that I dream my dreams and am continuously existent through sleep just as through waking, is entirely mistaken.

Exactly. The dream ego is a concept. The waking ego is also a concept. Their common reality lies in the underlying background, awareness.

Then the dream ego, the person in the dream to whom all the action happens, and who perceives everything else in the dream world, has no connection with the waking ego?

Exactly.

64

What would you say to people who think that there is an intimate connection between these two egos, and who attempt to work out the meaning of dreams for their life situation. Is there any access to the dream state while one is in the waking state?

To these persons, I would say, "Good luck!" because there is no connection between the two states other than through consciousness. So, it is a futile attempt which is bound to fail. Coming back to your original statement, ". . . we are the dreamer who appears in our dreams at night," I would say that we are not the dreamer *in* our dreams, we are the dreamer *of* all our dreams, including the so-called waking state which is another dream. So, we are the ultimate dreamer.

So, we dream not only each dream but the dreamer within each dream.

Exactly. We are the dreamer of all the dreamers in all the dreams.

You say that liberation is the death of the ego. How can we destroy the ego?

Who is going to destroy the ego? The ego? The ego sees itself as an obstacle and wants to get rid of itself as the obstacle, right?

It would seem so, but I can't imagine that the ego can commit suicide.

Exactly! There is no way the ego can get rid of itself. So, what are we going to do about it?

That is the question.

Don't do anything! Leave it alone! Just see it for what it is, like a cloud in the sky or a flower in the garden, an object. That is what it is, an object made out of a thought, the I-concept together with an attribute, which is a limitation, such as: I am a man, I am a father, I am young. All the qualities that have been attributed to you by your surroundings have created this so-called entity. So, simply be aware of it. See it for what it is. There is no need to kill it. On the contrary, welcome it, love it. As soon as you welcome it, it is neutralized.

What do you mean by non-duality?

Non-duality means there are not two things, like subject and object, man and woman, good and evil. There is no plurality. Any pair of opposites, from this perspective, is a figment of our imagination. Reality is non-dual. When we seemingly see an object, there is no object seen and there is no seer of it; there is only seeing. Seeing is awareness. Similarly, when we think, there is no thought and there is no thinker; there is only thinking. Thinking is awareness. Awareness, our real nature, is the only thing that is, if we can still speak of a thing; a thing that knows itself by itself.

If there is no plurality, then everything I know, have known, or could ever know is unreal. Do you actually mean to imply this, and, if you do, could you elaborate?

Everything we know is reality. We cannot know anything other than reality, awareness. Everything we know is awareness. Everything other than awareness is a mere hypothesis, a mere illusion . . .

Can I interject for a moment? You said, "Everything other than awareness." Is there anything else?

No, because if you claim that there is anything else, you carry the burden of proof. You are free to claim that there is such a thing as a unicorn, but you still have to bring me one.

This is true, but many people would say that, although there is no unicorn, there are horses, and they will bring you one.

So?

What have they brought you?

When we see an object, such as a horse, at the time of seeing, even the concept of a horse doesn't come in; even the image, the shape of the horse as a whole doesn't come in. The shape as a whole is a sophisticated mentation that arises after many glances have been taken in succession, after visual information has been processed bit by bit.

That is true. The retina doesn't have horse receptors.

I would even say that the retina at the time of perception is also a creation of your imagination. There is only awareness, from moment to moment. If an object is seen from this perspective, then we can say that this object is real. There is nothing wrong with objects, as long as we understand their true nature, as long as we understand them to be mere appearances on a background of awareness. They don't have any reality of their own. That is what is meant by non-duality.

So, objects, as we ordinarily take them to be, are completely imaginary. There are no objects that exist by themselves outside of awareness.

In this regard, there is nothing wrong with the perception. What is wrong is the misconception that follows: that I was there during the perception as a person, as the perceiver of this object, and that this object exists regardless of whether or not it is perceived. This is the basic error, which we call ignorance. It is not a pejorative term. It simply qualifies this superimposition of an external world made out of objects, and of a concomitant subject as the perceiver of that world. Ignorance refers to this division into two elements, which is the origin of all diversity.

Ignorance, in fact, refers to duality.

Exactly.

So, in reality, there are not two. Non-duality refers to reality, and the fact is that there is no plurality anywhere.

Exactly.

৯৹

What is death?

At the physical level, death is the dissolution, the disappearance of an object. It is the counterpart of birth. The interval between birth and death is called existence. The existence of the body is similar to the existence of any other physical object. It has a beginning in time, called birth, and an end in time, called death. Like the head and the tail of a cat, birth and death are inseparable.

At the level of the mind, death is the end of a mentation, when it disappears in its source, the background, consciousness. This disappearance is the counterpart of an appearance. These subtle objects, these mentations are time-dependent, as are the gross objects at the physical level. The difference is that physical objects are solely made out of perceptions, whereas mentations can be perceptions or thoughts. To put it into mathematical terms, the gross world can be seen as a subset of the subtle world.

Are you saying that the physical world is embedded in the mental world?

Yes. The distinction we make between two kinds of mentations, perceptions and thoughts, creates two different worlds, the physical world and the psychological world. Both of them are subsets, subuniverses of the subtle universe which is made out of mentations. (This perspective, that the so-called physical world is, in fact, subtle, is the foundation of the philosophical school known as idealism.) However, this understanding is still relative. We have to go beyond it and understand that between two mentations, we are, as the background. Any mentation takes birth out of, exists in, and dies into this background of awareness, our true nature.

If the background, which remains when any mentation ends, and I include within mentation sensations, is what we are, then there is no death.

Exactly! When we take our stand in the background, there is no death. At the relative levels, there is death: at the physical level, there is death at the end of the body; at the subtle level, there is death from moment to moment, at the end of a perception or a thought; at the ultimate level, there is only timeless continuity.

It seems to follow that the certainty that everyone has about their upcoming death, and the fear they have, is the consequence of having constituted themselves as a object . . .

Exactly.

. . . which necessarily has an end . . .

Exactly.

. . . and if they did not do this, they would not see death?

Yes. They would be free of fear. Fear comes from the notion of being a separate entity, either a physical entity identified with the body or a subtle entity identified with the mind. When we identify ourselves with life itself (and by life, I don't mean existence, a span in time between birth and death, but the core of our being, the timeless background), or rather, when we stop identifying ourselves with anything limited, with an object, be it gross or subtle, there is no death. So, to understand death, one first has to understand life. Then the question about death appears in a different light.

You characterized objects as having a beginning and an end, a birth and a death, and you said these were like the head and the tail of a single cat. We have seen through what you just said that for one who takes his stand in awareness, there is no death. Would it follow that there is no birth? Is one who takes his stand there eternal and outside of time?

We are timeless. There is nobody who takes his stand there other than the awareness that has always been there. In order to take a stand there, the person has to disappear. Nobody can take a stand there. We have always been there. We have always been who we are, and this spiritual essence transcends our humanity.

৶

What would you say to someone who finds it difficult to accept that happiness is his real nature, because he is unhappy much of the time?

I would say, "You know somehow that happiness exists. If you had no intuition of it, no taste or experience of it, you wouldn't even use the word . . ."

Yes, he couldn't ask you about it.

". . . you wouldn't even be able to say, 'I am unhappy,' because unhappiness directly refers to happiness. In order to be aware of your unhappiness, you must somehow feel happiness."

Or, he might say, "have felt happiness."

Well, there must still remain some residue of it, not as memory, but as reality, to enable him to experience his current dissatisfaction. Otherwise, his experience would be neutral.

Why couldn't his current dissatisfaction arise from his comparing the difference between the memory of a happy time and an unhappy present?

Because memory relates to objects only, to events. Although the alleged reason for my dissatisfaction is the unaffordability of the red Ferrari on display at the dealership, the memory of former happy times behind the wheel could not be the primary reason for my dissatisfaction, because I have never owned a Ferrari. A deeper inquiry is, therefore, needed.

Our dissatisfaction doesn't originate from the absence of the desired object, but from another source: from a compelling sense of lack within ourselves; the lack of something unknown, yet somehow forefelt. If we totally welcome this feeling, instead of doing what we usually do, go out, see a movie, or call up a friend, in an attempt to escape the situation, we would see this lack gradually lose its dynamism and evolve into a peaceful non-experience. This peace comes directly from our true nature. It has always been available. Our sense of lack was our real being reminding us of its presence when we were seeking happiness outside, in the objective world. When we understand this, and open ourselves to our inner core, this lack, as if by magic, changes into causeless bliss.

Are you happy all of the time?

I am happiness, you are happiness, awareness is happiness.

6

John Doe, the Actor

I would like to know if you have seen your original nature.

Why would you like to know that?

I would like to know because I think that a person who has seen his original nature could be a teacher for me.

Your teacher has to be discovered in your heart. You have to find out by yourself. When you find out, you discover your real nature.

In fact, there is no teacher. There is a teacher only for as long as one takes oneself to be a student. In the same way, as long as an infant needs breast-feeding there is a breast-feeding mother. But, from the vantage point of the so-called teacher there is no such distinction. There is only welcoming, oneness, happiness.

The student and teacher are one and the same.

Absolutely.

I just read an article in a publication on yoga. The thrust of it was that gurus and teachers are, perhaps, the biggest impediment on the planet. The author suggested that we retain our personal freedom and simply find out who we are, instead of remaining a student and following somebody around, reading books, or ceaselessly looking for another teacher.

As long as you take yourself for a personal entity, you may assume two positions: one in which you want someone to help you, or one in which you want to find the truth by yourself, and don't want to be taught. Even if someone is helping, you need to, at least, complete the work. That is why a good teacher doesn't give you everything already made, pre-digested. He gives you stuff to work on and understand by yourself. This universal principle applies to any kind of teaching, including spiritual teaching. If you take either of these two positions you are right. In the first case, because the desire to find a spiritual teacher comes from a deep desire to find your Self, and in the second case, because there is a desire for independence, for autonomous understanding, which emanates from your own autonomy, your own independence. As long as you don't feel a desire for a teacher, don't worry about it. Everything, every person, every event in your life is your teacher. At some point something you read, or hear, or a person you meet, may provide an insight which will make it clear to you that there is a possibility to live free of the notion of being a person—to live knowingly in your freedom and your happiness. In the beginning, you may be open to this possibility of a creative life, then doubts may arise. In this case, you may want to meet someone who lives in freedom. It was in this spirit that I started looking for a spiritual teacher in my early years, and I didn't regret it. Another reason for seeking a teacher is to find answers to questions you may have. There are many good reasons to meet a teacher. But, in fact, there is only one: to meet yourself— your Self. You are looking for your Self. Your Self is not limited by, or to, this body and this mind. Your Self is immense, beautiful, and immortal. Be open to that possibility, be open to the source of all possibilities.

You spoke of the possibility of not being a person, but being free and happy. Could you please elaborate?

The actor on stage who plays Hamlet today, Macbeth tomorrow, and King Lear the next day doesn't take himself for Hamlet, Macbeth, or King Lear. He takes himself for John Doe, the actor. But, this doesn't prevent him from being Hamlet, Macbeth, or King Lear on stage. When you know that you are awareness, and not a man or a woman, a spouse or a parent, this knowledge doesn't prevent you from playing all of these parts one after another. But, since these parts aren't permanent, they aren't you, because what you are is continuous. These various characters you play are like garments. You put them on, you take them off, and you get a new garment. What you are is always present.

Does the playing of the roles somehow contribute to our identification with a personal entity? Is there a reason why we are playing roles?

You can play whatever role the current circumstances in your life require, but without identifying yourself with it, with the personal. Now, if you are asking if there is any reason for identifying yourself with a personal entity, the answer is no. There is no good reason. Just don't do that. Don't even say that there is no good reason. Just don't do that.

The second question was, "Is there a reason why we are playing roles?" Well, it would be boring otherwise. Diversity is part of beauty. It is a celebration. What we are, our true nature, is not a blank. It isn't nothingness. It contains everything. Everything is our Self, therefore, your Self from moment to moment.

Everything you see, everything you touch, everything you think is you. Just after the thought, after the perception, after the feeling, you say, "I was there as a person and I was having this thought, this feeling, this perception." But, that isn't true, because at the time of the thought, feeling, or perception there was no thinker, feeler, or perceiver, and there was no object thought, felt, or perceived. There was only thinking, feeling, perceiving. So, from moment to moment there is only oneness. And this is what you are. This is the real you. As such, you are not here or there. "I am here," is a thought. When you eliminate this thought, where are you?

I was with you up until the last part.
Are you with yourself?

What do you mean?
Are you with yourself? Or is your Self separate from you?

I am separate.
You are separate from yourself?

I am working on myself.
How do you know that you are separate from yourself?

It is a long story.
How do you know now that you are now separate from yourself without going into the past? Not yesterday or tomorrow, but now. Are you separate from yourself? On what basis can you say that?

Keep going because I think I am . . .
Try to find whether you are really separate from yourself. Try to find out for sure. What I feel is that I am always with myself. I am my best companion. How could I be separate from myself?

Maybe it is just that I think I am separate.
Yes. But, where does your thought that you are separate appear?

In myself.
Right. So you are not separate from yourself.

I don't know, I have to think about it.
Think about it.

So separateness is something we do in thinking, not in reality?
Absolutely.

If we could all stop thinking we would all be very happy.

We don't need to stop thinking. We can't actually end thinking as a result of effort, because the effort itself would involve thinking. There is a story about a king who was very ill. He sent for a famous physician and told him, "Cure me or I'll have your head cut off." Seeing that the king was dying, the physician said, "I can save you, but you have to follow my instructions carefully, otherwise the medicine will be ineffective." The king agreed. The physician gave him some medicine and asked him not to think about a gray monkey whenever he took it. Of course, this turned out to be impossible. So, the king died and the physician saved his own life. This story tells you that if you try to stop thinking, your trying requires thinking, so you can never achieve your goal.

Do thoughts stop? I guess what I am trying to express is that thoughts are helpful in our role-playing, but don't necessarily help us to be who we are.

The kind of thoughts which are not useful are thoughts which derive from the notion of being a person. Such thoughts bring about hatred, separateness, fury, desire, and so on. They are conducive to negative emotions. If I am convinced that I am this limited body-mind, born a few years ago and bound to die within a few years, there is no way I can prevent the myriad thoughts which originate from this belief from coming up. If I make an effort to prevent them from coming up, pressure will build up inside me, and I may end up in jail or in a mental institution. There is no way of preventing these thoughts from arising as long as their root has not been cut. If I want to get rid of the leaves of a tree, because they are littering my front yard, I can try to remove the leaves one by one, but next spring they will be back again. The real solution is to cut the trunk or, better, uproot the tree. The root of these thoughts and negative emotions is the notion that I am a personal entity, that I am separate. The uprooting of the tree is the understanding that my actual experience, the eternal now, is devoid of such a separation.

How do people make the shift of consciousness from identifying with their separate personality to becoming aware of the truth?

There is nothing the person can do to see that "personness" is a fake. The person persistently adheres to his identity as a person, but there are moments of freedom from this identity. In these moments there is an opportunity to take some distance and have a glimpse of this presence which we all are—awareness.

What is our most precious good? It isn't any part of our body. This is evidenced by the fact that people will submit to having a body part amputated, if necessary to save their life. Our most precious good is not even the body in its totality. What we really love is consciousness. The real question is: Is consciousness in the body or is the body in consciousness? We have been conditioned by our surroundings, by our teachers, by the prevalent materialism, to believe that our body is in the world, our brain is in the body, and consciousness is a function of the brain. From the vantage point of non-duality, the picture is just the opposite: The ultimate reality is awareness, within which there is the mind. The body, the thoughts, and the rest of the universe all appear in the mind. Now, how am I going to decide, from these two positions, which one is true? It is important to understand with our logical apparatus, the mind, that this question can't be decided by the mind. If I choose one of these positions rather than the opposite, it is a belief, an act of faith. If I see that clearly, I am already free from the concept that I am in the world, that I am my body. I understand that existence in the world is an act of faith, not an absolute truth, and I am now open to the other possibility. The mind can't decide because it knows only that which is within itself. What is beyond the mind cannot be known by the mind. All it can do is understand that it cannot decide. When it understands that it can't find the ultimate answer, it becomes quiet. In this stillness there is the possibility for our true nature to take us. We can't take it. We can only be open and welcome it.

The past few months, I have been meditating at night before I go to sleep. I have been going through, "I am not my body, I am not my mind, I am not my feelings," and thinking about it. Then the question, "Who am I?" arises. Everything then comes to a screeching halt, and it is very alarming. My mind can't figure it out, and I haven't been able to move beyond that. I see clearly that

I am not my mind, my body, or my feelings, but the, "Who am I?" part is a big blank. It is like there is nothing there, and then I experience a very alarming feeling. My mind just can't get it. So, are you saying that when the mind understands that it can't get it, something else opens up?

In the process you are describing you eliminate what you are not, but there is still a dynamism in you. You are starting this process with a goal in mind. It is the highest end, to realize your true nature. However, it is still a goal. As long as there is the slightest trace of intent in you the door remains closed. That is why it is so difficult to learn and understand how to meditate without help, and to establish oneself, without proper guidance, in the correct attitude of welcoming.

I have a friend who lives in Europe. I have never met him, but we write to one another through the Internet, and he asks questions that I try to answer. He wanted to know the proper attitude for knowingly being the truth. This is virtually impossible to convey through words only. Finally, after a few exchanges, I advised him to attend the talks of a dear friend of mine who gives dialogues in his country, and to simply sit in his presence. That will teach him, because in the presence of someone who is free from the ego we spontaneously take the proper attitude, without knowing it, and we become free. One who is free from the notion of being a personal entity is not limited in space. He lives in an expansion, in welcoming, and when awareness in you, through a very subtle antenna, detects his field of welcoming, you start opening up. Your own space starts expanding. You might not notice it in the beginning. After my first meeting with Jean Klein, the feeling I had was not, "He is a realized person." I thought, "What a nice gentleman! What a good friend he would be!" So, you aren't grabbed by violence. You are grabbed through this welcoming. In this openness you aren't afraid because you are totally accepted. Nothing in you is judged or evaluated. When you leave him you have the perfume of this presence and now you know how to meditate. This fragrance of welcoming is all you need. When you are in listening you are not going anywhere. You don't know anything. All agitation stops. Then, there is an unfolding. You find yourself more and more in this expansion, and one day this sticky little thing you thought you were just falls off like a tick. Then you discover your beauty, your eternity. You know and are what you really desired. It is beyond the plus and the minus. It is beyond measure—absolute! That is what you are. You are that beauty.

It is ironic that the progress toward consciousness is unconscious. It unfolds slowly without you knowing it.

The mind doesn't know it, but it is not unconscious. Would you say that the fish is unconscious of being in the water?

He knows.

When he is taken out of the water he knows it as an objective perception. While being in the water, in his natural state, he isn't objectively conscious of the presence of the water. There is no need for that, because he is one with it, and knows his happiness. How do you know that you are happy? The moment you say, "I am happy" you are no longer happy. When you are happy you know it, but you don't know it objectively. You don't know it as you know what you had for breakfast. You know it somehow, but through a different channel. This channel is very important. The channel through which you know that you are happy is the channel through which you know yourself. Find this channel. In other words, when you are happy, know that this happiness emanates from your true Self, not from something, not from an event, not from an object, not from a person. That is all you need. You don't need to understand everything that is said here. There is only one thing to understand, so just take this one and you'll be fine. That is called the path of happiness.

What is the way to get there if it isn't meditating and finding your true self?

There are a thousand and one types of meditation. So when you ask that question, I don't know what you mean.

I only know what I have learned here. I am new to this.

OK.

78

What I am learning now is just to try to release my mind. I don't really know enough to give you an example.

There is only one way to get there. It is through desiring it. If you have no desire for it, you won't get it, and you won't be frustrated. However, if you desire it, it will find a way to come to you, because in this desire there is already the fulfillment of all desires. If you desire this happiness, which is causeless, which doesn't come from any object, let this desire be your guide.

Don't I have to read some books or find a teacher to arouse this desire? It shouldn't just be a concept. Believing that I am not my body, my personality, or my personal history is one thing, but I want to experience it. Being around a charismatic teacher is either really going to get me there or leave me in a cult. I would like the help, but I can't see myself going off alone with all my books, sitting in a cave, and going mad with desire.

Life may prove you wrong. To find the truth you have to move away from any exclusion. If you say, "I am not going to find it there," think twice. The desire for the truth, being born from a glimpse of the truth, doesn't come from the person. It comes from grace. There appears to be a personal entity with a desire for the truth moving on a gradual path toward truth, but, in fact, the truth was there in the beginning, the truth is along the path, and the truth is at the end of the path. The truth *is*—before the beginning and after the end. There is only the truth. There is only grace. Once you understand that, you don't look for it in the future or in the past, because it is here and now. Your current sensation, your current thought, your current perception emanates from your awareness, rests in your awareness, falls in your awareness. The substance it is made out of is your awareness. So, everything is your awareness. Everything is you; everything you see; everything you understand. You are the fabric out of which this universe is made. And it is created in the present. It was not created in the past. Everything is created from moment to moment, always new. Like fireworks, this universe is a celebration and you are the spectator contemplating the eternal Fourth of July of your absolute splendor.

Someone mentioned feeling alarmed when she got to a certain point, and other people have described being terrified at the point where they were just ready to open up to this awareness. What causes these overwhelming reactions?

In these circumstances you have the opportunity to see what you are not: the ego. The ego is not a single thought, it is a recurrent thought pattern which, like frozen yogurt, comes in various flavors, such as, I am a mother, I am a father, I am my body. The ego is also made out of feelings, such as, fear, boredom, dissatisfaction, and a sense of lack. When you feel boredom, you touch the tip of the iceberg. If you welcome this feeling, you move into deeper waters as it becomes fear and even panic. Remain in welcoming. It is a test of the intensity of your desire for the truth. At some point, the desire for the truth becomes so intense that you are willing to die for it. When there is a readiness to give up everything, the fear will instantaneously disappear and the eternal consciousness will reveal itself in all its glory. That will be the end of the ego and of the problems that are associated with it.

You speak of the Self and also of consciousness. Is there any separation between the Self and the whole consciousness? Is there some part of that awareness that is separate? Are we reincarnated? Do we have a personality apart from the entire consciousness?

You know that you are conscious, but you don't know yet that your awareness, which is you, goes beyond the limitations of your body-mind. We all share this awareness. It is our common good. All you have to do is to be open to that possibility. As long as you want to remain an ego, you will remain as such. Be happy with it, if you can. But, there may come a time when you feel dissatisfaction, and understand that this constant drive to seek pleasure and avoid pain is what keeps you in misery.

7

A Real Teacher Doesn't Take Himself for a Teacher

How can a seeker know that he has met an authentic teacher and not merely someone who is offering a new philosophy or a new version of an old philosophy?

There will be, at first, the intuition that this person may be the one he was seeking to help him along the path. Then, at some point, through the words and gestures of the teacher, through the modulations of his voice and the look in his eyes, or more importantly, through his silent presence (because everything in an authentic teacher speaks of the truth, comes from the truth, and invites the truth), a fusion in the heart will occur that will give the seeker the total conviction that he has met the one for whom he was looking. In this real meeting with his teacher, he meets the ultimate friendliness and intelligence they both have in common: he meets himself.

A real teacher doesn't take himself for a teacher. He doesn't claim to be different from his student. He doesn't try to manipulate him. He leaves him with a feeling of enhanced freedom, of increased autonomy. He is not a father figure, nor does he try to convert the student. His behavior is a perfect example of humility and devotion to the truth.

More than his words, his humility and his genuine innocence convince the seeker, deep in his heart, that he has met the teacher for whom he was looking.

How can one know he is in the presence of an inauthentic teacher?

If there is a lack of clarity, if the teacher manifests personal emotions or feelings, such as attachment to his students, then you can know. I said earlier that a fusion in the heart has to occur in the presence of the teacher in order to bring about the total certitude of his authenticity. By "fusion in the heart," I wasn't referring to any emotional state, such as the states that can be experienced along a path of devotion, but rather to a non-event that results from absolute clarity of the mind. This comes first. Then, and only then, is there a fusion in the heart. In the absence of clarity, there is still a person-to-person relationship between a teacher who may be a holy person, but still a person, and a student who is bound to remain a student for as long as the teacher remains a person, which may be for a long time.

ℒ

Is it necessary to be intelligent to realize the ultimate?

It is necessary to be highly intelligent. However, what I call higher intelligence is different from common intelligence. Common intelligence is a cerebral ability that, for instance, enables an individual possessing it to obtain a postgraduate degree from a good university. It implies the ability to deal logically with complex and abstract questions that involve a large amount of data. It is a function of the brain.

Higher intelligence, on the other hand, originates from the supreme intelligence, our true nature. It enables us to understand simplicity, unity. Common intelligence is a deductive process in time; higher intelligence is an instantaneous intuition that comes directly from the timeless. A very simple being can know the truth, whereas a highly educated one can fail to know it.

ℒ

Is higher reasoning affected by the physical state of the body, by the use of drugs, illness, or by the kind of food one eats?

The source of higher reasoning is not, the process of higher reasoning may be. The search for the truth, this investigation about our real nature, requires a very sharp mind. The use or abuse of drugs or alcohol may impair the mind's natural alertness.

If someone is earnestly seeking, will he necessarily change his eating habits?

Real intelligence doesn't exclude anything. It applies to the whole of our life. It affects everything, including the way we smile and the way we eat. These changes in our habits are a result of understanding. The body-mind is our instrument, our vehicle. We have to take good care of it and put the right kind of fuel into it.

What is the significance of vegetarianism?

Obviously, to think that a change in our eating habits would take us closer to the truth reflects a misunderstanding . . .

Of course, but I was asking the opposite . . .

If a change in habits comes as a result of understanding, that is a different question. This understanding comes from seeing situations as they are. When we feel in unity with our animal companions, compassion prevents us from being an accomplice to their suffering. We may also notice that someone we trust, a spiritual friend, for instance, is a vegetarian. Since we are open-minded, we can try this new diet and notice how it affects our body, immediately after the meals, and also after a few months. We may notice changes in the color and texture of our skin, or in the feeling of heaviness or lightness in our body. We can experiment in this way and make an autonomous decision.

ॐ

Many people who begin to explore their own nature get caught up with the notion of reincarnation. Could we go into this question?

Who is there to reincarnate? The ego?

They would reply, yes, the person, the mind.

I would suggest that they inquire, "Who is there?" which means, "Who am I?" and find out whether there is an entity that can eventually reincarnate. Reincarnation is to the idealist what death is to the materialist. To the materialist who inquires, "What is death?" we can put the question, "Who is there to die?" Similarly, in the case of the idealist for whom the body is part of the mind, and for whom the mind does not necessarily die when the body dies, the question is, "How can I escape from the endless cycle of birth and death?" This question can be met by asking, "Who is there to go through this reincarnation process?"

The answer, the living answer to this question, leads the seeker to the understanding that the ego is a mere illusion. He then finds himself beyond death and beyond the infernal cycle of death and rebirth.

ॐ

If the past does not really exist, what is the nature of memory?

Memory is made of records of past events, of objects. A personal memory, or recollection, tells us that we were present as awareness during a past event. The same consciousness witnessed the past event and is now witnessing its recollection. In fact, the recollection only confirms the reality of awareness, the unchanging presence behind the impermanent events. If this is understood, the interval between the past event and its current recollection is seen as awareness. If we believe that the events exist independently from awareness, identifying awareness with some appearing object, a body-mind, the same interval is seen as having a consciousness-independent reality. We call it time. To sum it up: when we grant reality to objects, to an external world, time seems to exist as an interval between two events; when awareness is seen as real, there is no time, there is only awareness.

If there is only the present, and there are only current upcoming thoughts, what is the meaning behind some of them coming up, from time to time, identified as memories, as recollections of something that occurred at some point in the past?

There is no meaning. Time and space are part of the creation of this illusory world. It could equally be said that their sole meaning is to celebrate the ultimate.

So, the fact that some thoughts arise labeled as memories is simply a part of this huge artifice?

Exactly. It is a huge artifice, a very well thought out one, but nevertheless an artifice. Our dreams are also very well thought out, very sophisticated.

That is true. In fact, we have memories in dreams, which we see upon awakening, never happened at all.

Exactly. During the time span of a dream, which from the perspective of the waking state lasts for a few minutes, we can dream of events that allegedly happened twenty years ago in the dream. When we wake up, it becomes obvious that these events never had a proper space-time frame in which they could have existed, and thus are mere illusions.

The Christian church holds poverty to be a virtue. Is there any relation between wealth or poverty, and realization?

Meister Eckhart, who was a Christian, taught that spiritual poverty, real poverty, is freedom from the I-concept. This real poverty, which originates from understanding, liberates us from attachment. The I-concept, with its train of fears, desires, and attachments, is the problem, not our material possessions.

ৎ

Krishna Menon, a great teacher of this perspective, defined language as the art of concealing thought, and thought as the art of concealing truth. Could you expand on these definitions?

We could draw an analogy in which truth is the naked body, thought is a first layer of clothes covering the body, and words are a second layer of clothes veiling both the thoughts and the body. Of course, we run the risk of taking the appearance, the veil, for the reality, the body. In this sense, thoughts and words may divert our attention from truth.

However, there are also words and thoughts which direct our attention toward truth. These words and thoughts can be compared with the clothes a beautiful woman wears, making her body even more attractive by drawing attention toward her harmonious proportions. Truth is always present, but we may forget its presence, and these kinds of words and thoughts remind us of its presence. Such are the sayings of the teacher: they directly point toward truth. They come from beauty, they point toward beauty, and they have the power to take us back to their source.

ৎ

What is the nature of bondage? Who is bound? What binds him?

Bondage consists of considering oneself to be someone who is bound, a limited entity.

It seems extraordinary that such a simple thing, a person believing himself to be bound, could generate this enormous experience that we call life.

To see oneself as bound does not generate life. Life has an existence of its own. Life is autonomous. To see oneself as a person is what generates misery.

But doesn't life give rise to the experience of being an individual inserted into the world?

Yes, but our experience, life itself, is not the product of the person. The person is part of the picture. As any element of the picture, it can be there, or it can be absent. One may think that the picture looks better in its absence, but in any case one doesn't draw the picture.

Why doesn't a sage use his understanding to work in an obvious way, in an open way, for the benefit of humanity?

All sages do work for the benefit of humanity. They simply don't advertise their work. They don't need recognition. We don't know they are sages. Only a few become openly teachers of truth. A sage has the most efficient, the most powerful impact on the rest of mankind, through his mere presence, through the transmission of the ultimate truth. He is like a beacon in the night, a flame that illuminates the world.

ॐ

In the context of seeking the truth, what is the meaning and purpose of surrender?

People often think that surrender means to renounce wealth, sexuality, or objects. Such a renunciation might be useful but it could also be a hindrance. Real surrender takes place when we cease to take ourself for a separate entity, an object. This renunciation seems, at first sight, limited in scope and too simple, but it is, in fact, the ultimate surrender. Such a giving up has no purpose, it comes from the deep understanding that our true nature, consciousness, is free from all limitations. From this perspective, surrender means to see the limitations for what they are: mere concepts superimposed onto our real being, which is limitless.

It seems easy for a person to give up an idea, a possession, or the opportunity to have an experience. These things are easy, because the person can do them by choice. But, for the person to give himself up is quite another matter, and it seems to me like it is anything but easy. It can't be done in the way the other things can be done.

Of course, the person cannot give himself up. The person is always looking for something. The person wants to exchange . . .

Make a deal?

Make a deal. The person is willing to exchange wealth or anything else for a greater good, but can't just give himself up. Real surrender comes from love, from grace, when there is an insight into the supreme. Everything else becomes relative, being important only as a modality, as an aspect of the ultimate. From this perspective, surrender is our natural state, the absence of an owner. It means to literally disown everything, every object. It is this surrender to which Meister Eckhart refers when he says that a man who is "poor in spirit" is one who owns nothing, wants nothing, and knows nothing.

ço

How would you characterize the difference between listening to the words of a sage in person, and reading his writings or his sayings? This is a question that is important for truth-seekers who don't, or feel they don't, have access to a sage.

Words can be misleading. If the words of a sage are received without his presence, the reader has to conceptualize them, because he doesn't know any other way of knowing. He will arrive at concepts that are more subtle and, in a sense, closer to the truth. But, in practice, in most cases, in order to have a glimpse of truth itself, the presence of the sage is necessary in the beginning. In his presence conceptualizing comes to an end and is replaced by experience. After this experience, the seeker, reading the words of the sage or simply remembering his presence, will be brought back to the timeless glimpse he had during the first meeting. The words no longer refer to something unknown. Although he can't grasp or visualize this "something" in his mind, the words point toward what he now knows to be his own reality, his intimate experience.

How is that?

Because he knows it now. Jean Klein used the following example: If you have never eaten a mango, the word mango won't suggest any flavor to you. If somebody describes the taste and texture of the mango as being like those of a sweet peach or apricot, you will have a more accurate idea of the mango than if you visualize it as a carrot. But, it will still be a concept. After having once tasted the real thing, you know.

ᘛ

Is it possible to clearly see or know the interval between two thoughts or two perceptions, and, if that is so, is it possible to prolong that interval?

Is it possible to see this interval? Yes. Not to see it as an object, but to be it, to be alive in it. Is it possible to prolong it? Here a misconception arises, because this interval is not in time. How could the timeless be prolonged? This question originates from the desire to prolong a pleasurable experience, a samadhi. Such is the goal of a yogin who is in the business of achieving the cessation of all mind activities in order to experience the peace that comes with this cessation. The problem is that when he comes out of his samadhi he wants to find out how to get there again, and remain in it longer. Thinking so, doing so, he remains a prisoner in the chains of time.

So, even the notion of interval is wrong here. A succession of thoughts with gaps would imply a temporal succession, which is a misconception.

Yes, exactly.

It is not an interval.

Time is the substance of the mind, in the same way as space-time is the substance of the physical body and of the world. From the vantage point of the mind, this gap is an interval between two mentations; from the vantage point of the interval itself, it is the silent background, our timeless presence. From the vantage point of time, the gap has a beginning and an end, and thus an alleged duration, which gives rise to the question about its prolongation. If rugs and pieces of furniture are on the floor, at first sight there are objects with pieces of floor in between; but upon examination, it turns out that a single floor is the common support of all the objects.

The existence of the interval between thoughts is made obvious by pointing out that thoughts could not be continuous, because, if they were, there would not be thoughts, there would be one long thought. Each thought, thus, begins and ends. The fact that each thought has a duration, a beginning and an end, implies the notion of an interval. Is there a more direct way of knowing the interval other than this argument?

Of course, because we can't know it through reasoning. We can only infer its existence in this way. All we can say is, "It makes sense" or "Why not?" This is already important, because it puts to rest the notion that there is not such a thing as pure consciousness, and we are now open to the possibility that we stand as awareness between mentations. However, between the conceptual inference of its existence and the actual experience of being awareness, there is the same difference as the one between the planning of Columbus' trip to India and the discovery of America. This clarification through reasoning is useful. It erases the doubts of the seeker and leaves him open to the possibility that there is something beyond the mind.

Then, as a result of the glimpse he has in the presence of his instructor, something changes in him. These intervals between thoughts are no longer an absence, or a blank, they are pregnant with our presence. They are alive, they have an unexpected fullness. They are that with which he is really in love.

ॐ

If consciousness lies beyond opposites, and everything we have ever known lies within the field of opposites, within conceptualizing, how can we come to know consciousness?

It is not true to say that everything we have ever known lies within the realm of concepts. We have simply superimposed a net of concepts onto the known. The problem is not with what we know, but rather with the concepts we have about what we know. Otherwise, it would not be possible to have any access to the truth if it were radically separate from us. Nothing separates us from the truth, with the possible exception of our imagination. When we stop projecting a non-real separation, we find our Self to be what we have always been, where we have always been, and the so-called world finds its own place as an extension of the ultimate.

In a sense, this question arises from a wish to know consciousness conceptually, otherwise we would not accept that we know it.

We would like to know it objectively, as we think we know the world, or our body, or our thoughts. In fact, we never know objects, because there are no objects. There is only a continuum of consciousness, there is only one thing.

Does art have any function in daily life or in the pursuit of truth?

Art points toward beauty; art speaks to us about beauty. Beauty, truth, and love are one and the same. They are attributes of the ultimate. So art points toward the ultimate. That is its function.

How does art do that? How can a painting or a book, which are physical objects, be especially pointing toward the ultimate? Don't other objects point toward the ultimate?

Let's first consider the second part of the question. In principle, any object points toward the ultimate. But, to reveal the ultimate is not the function of all objects. Unlike most objects, a work of art refers to beauty directly, specifically, by design, so to speak. It uses the five senses as a vehicle, be it the auditory sense in the case of music or

91

the visual sense in the case of plastic arts (although it could be argued that a piece of art in fact makes use of all the five senses; that there is rhythm in a painting and color in a concerto). A piece of art is a physical, sensorial object which has the power to bring the seer or the listener to the ultimate.

Real art comes from the ultimate, from a vision; from the spirit, as Beethoven would say; from God, as Bach would say. Of course, technical skills are required to transform this vision into a physical shape, to translate it into the sensory language. When we listen to it, when we see it, we go through the various stages in reverse order. We move back from the sensory message to the original subtle intuition, and from there back to its source, where we are left alone in our own splendor.

8

There Is Nothing That Is Not Him

What is enlightenment?

Enlightenment is the experience of our true nature, which is made possible by the deep understanding of what we are not. Just as there is no need to light a candle in a room in which the curtains have been opened to let in the sunlight, nothing further is necessary once the mistaken identification with what we are not has been removed, and our true nature shines it its eternal glory.

Enlightenment, then, is the leaving behind of a thought that we are something, when, in fact, we are not.

Yes. It is knowingly standing as awareness disidentified from any limiting thought or feeling. From the vantage point of the person, from a relative vantage point, it is a hypothetical event in time and space, but this is a misconception originating from the person. From the vantage point of light, there is only light: There has always been and will always be only light. It is beyond time.

It seems like a paradox, because what you are saying implies that there couldn't be such a thing as an enlightened person. That would be a contradiction in terms.

Exactly.

Yet, I have the impression that some individuals are enlightened and others are not. Is this a misconception?

Of course it is a misconception. As long as you take yourself to be a person, you will see persons everywhere; some beautiful, some not; some enlightened, some not. Once you realize you are the Self, you will see the Self, and only the Self, everywhere. In other words, as long as the student takes himself for a student, for a personal entity, he also projects a personal entity onto his teacher. When he realizes that he and his teacher are one, there is no longer a student, there is no longer a teacher; there is only respectful friendliness, shared joy. Conceiving realization as an event in time is an obstacle to enlightenment. To the question, "When will I realize the truth?" the sage Atmananda Krishna Menon replied, "When the when ceases."

The statement that the world and our body are mere illusions comes as a shock to most Western thinkers. Could we explore this further?

First, let's understand that from the point of view of the witnessing consciousness, the body is a material object like any other. Along with the rest of the world as we actually know it, it is made out of sensory perceptions.

But, it isn't quite correct to say that the body, like any other object, is made out of sensations. These other objects are made out of matter, and they are revealed to us via sensations, via the sense organs, the mind, and awareness.

Yes. At this instant, the illusory aspect of the world comes in. When we say that the world is made out of matter, we already implicitly define the world not as the world we actually know, but as a concept. We replace an undeniable fact, our sensory experience of the world, by the unverifiable hypothesis of a world out there that exists independently of us.

In fact, by a concept of matter which is not only unknown, but in principle unknowable.

Even before the concept of matter, which is a concept for the physicist, there is the implicit notion that there is an external world which exists independently of awareness, which exists even when it isn't perceived.

Yes, and the theory of matter is a formal conceptualizing of this implicit understanding.

It is a refinement, a scientific theory that makes use of the pre-scientific concept of an external world.

You are saying that the notion of an external world made of matter is the beginning of the illusion, whereas for a Western thinker it is the beginning of the notion of reality.

It might be the beginning of the notion of reality, but not of the experience of reality. We don't need the notion of an external world to know that "we are," and to know that "there is something rather than nothing," as Heidegger would say. Reality is the primal fact, concepts are secondary. To think the other way around, even implicitly or inadvertently, is a big mistake. In this case, a notion creates an illusory reality. Even this erroneous notion in the mind of the thinker is the living proof of reality, because there is something rather than nothing, or quoting Parmenides, because "being is, and non-being is not." From this perspective, everything is reality, every object is seen in its oneness, without the notion of a subject seeing an object.

So, every object is not seen as an object.

Yes. In the words of the sufis of the School of Oneness, "there is nothing that is not Him." Everything is one and the same thing.

Why is the firm belief in an external world so widespread and so tenacious? Why are so few people able to even seriously question it?

The "Why?" takes us away. To know why there are so many people who think otherwise doesn't get us one inch closer to the truth. The real question is, "Is there a world without awareness?" If anyone claims that there is a reality that exists independently from consciousness, he carries the burden of proof.

In psychoanalytic theory, the function of the ego is to put one in touch with external reality. We have seen that there is no such reality. What becomes of an ego so defined?

This definition of the ego becomes meaningless. I would define the ego as a concept originating from the "I am" experience, pure being without attributes, the absolute certitude we have that we exist. When we conceptualize this experience, we call it "I" or "I am." There is nothing wrong with the pure concept "I am." The ego comes in the moment we say, "I am this or that," "I am a man," or "I am a parent." This superimposes a limitation onto something that, up until now, was limitless. The first step was the creation of the concept "I am" which directly refers to our most intimate experience. As long as there is no add-on to this concept, such as "I am a man," "I am happy," "I am unhappy," this concept can't maintain itself and brings us back to the "I am" experience.

So the concept appears in awareness . . .

It also refers to awareness, to reality. It originates from reality and brings us back to reality. We remain, so to speak, at home. But, the moment we say, "I am this or that" we create a division in reality . . .

Between the me and the not me?

Exactly, because if I am "this," I am not "not this." There is something that I am not. I have assigned a limit, a contour to my being. The ego is this contour. It defines two separate domains, creating duality.

So the ego is the first distinction, from which all others arise?

Precisely. This distinction, the ego, the dualizing thought, which has no real foundation, creates plurality. It is a larger definition of the ego than the division between the observer and the observed, which is one of its modalities.

It seems to me that defining the ego the way you have defined it simultaneously defines the world.

Absolutely. The body-mind complex and the world are two sides of the same coin, artificially created by the same dualizing thought out of what was, and still is, oneness.

ॐ

How can one know that a felt longing to know the truth isn't the ego still attempting to remain secure?

A real longing for the absolute, for the impersonal, does not come from the ego. We can feel our own earnestness involving the whole of our life. It isn't limited to our intellectual life, but manifests in all our daily actions and decisions: the kind of profession we have, the way we behave with our children, spouse, and friends. It has a deep impact on us. Our own genuineness, our earnestness, our longing are very well known to us.

Yes, that is true, but I was really asking about the other possibility: an intellectual pursuit, orchestrated by the ego, which takes over much of a person's life. People can suddenly, and continuously thereafter, spend much of their time talking and reading about these questions in a way that looks earnest, but is really just an academic interest.

What matters is the motivation. If the motivation is the absolute itself, there is genuineness. If I want to be acknowledged as an expert in non-dualism, make money, or be admired by others, if there is a personal motivation, there is no earnestness. There is only one motivation for a truth-lover, and that is truth itself. This motivation is not driven by the ego. Truth pulverizes the ego. How could the ego desire that?

ॐ

The mind arises in awareness, but awareness somehow acts through the mind. Could you clarify this interrelationship?

The mind is a concept which, like any other concept, refers to other concepts or to perceptions. In this case, the mind is seen as the container of all mentations. The mind is not an organ like the brain. It isn't perceived. It is only a concept. So, there actually is no mind; there is only the concept of a mind. What then is there? There are just thoughts and perceptions, or more precisely, mentations. A mentation originates from awareness and, sooner or later, dissolves into awareness. Thus, any mentation is awareness, in the same way as a gold ring, which originates from gold and later melts down into gold, is always only gold. So there is only awareness.

The interval between arising and dissolving is an apparent informing.

You can call it awareness with an object, with a form, or with a concept. But, it still is awareness. There is only one thing. Where has your question gone?

It has vanished. There can't be any interrelationship if there is only one.

What would you say to those who find your perspective either too theoretical, or too difficult to apply in their everyday life situations?

This perspective is the least theoretical of any. Theoretical means based on concepts. Non-dualism leads to a total disbelief in all concepts, so it is radically non-theoretical. Since the sage isn't interested in any theories, his vantage point is eminently practical. When confronted by a non-objective perspective, those who have been conditioned to understand in conceptual terms, by moving from one concept to another, fail to find a concept to grab onto, and attribute their failure to understand to the complexity or theoretical character of non-dualism. The only obstacle is their own beliefs, theories, and habits which prevent them from having the direct experience of their own real nature.

Don't worry if you don't understand every argument used by the instructor expounding this perspective, because each of them is one side, one face of the same truth. Any of these paths lead to the ultimate. You need only take one of them to get there and to stay there. In time, as you establish yourself in the single truth, all questions find their final answer. From the top of the mountain, looking down on the valleys, we can see all the paths leading to the summit: the one we have followed, and also many others we could have taken.

Coming back to the original point, a theoretical approach never leads to a fully satisfactory answer to any question. To the question, "Why A?" the theoretician answers, "Because B." Then the question, "Why B?" arises, to which he answers "Because C," and so on. He remains caught in the endless regression of causality.

It is clear that in assuming this perspective to be based on theoretical presuppositions, they have made a mistake. But have they made a mistake in thinking that it is very difficult? It certainly doesn't seem easy to transcend concepts.

It is very difficult. In fact, it is impossible for the ego to have a clear understanding of this perspective; but, it is easy for the heart to have an inkling of it. So I would tell them, "Let your heart be your guide. Whatever brings you a flash of joyful understanding, keep it, cherish it. Don't start from the negative side, from the 'I don't understand' side. Start with what you understand, with what makes you happy. There is no need to understand everything, because there is only one thing to understand: your permanent inner core. Only you can understand you. Only you can be you. You can't see you, you can't think you, because you are you." Isn't that simple?

What you are saying is very simple. However, life situations are far from simple. They are fast, difficult, and complex. How do you follow your heart in the midst of all that?

Then, it isn't what I am saying which is not simple . . .

No, it is their daily experience.

The concepts they have about themselves and the world are not simple. The non-dual perspective has to be explained in their own terms, in intellectual terms to the intellectual, and so on. The instructor, having in this manner established a bridge to communicate with them at their own level, will eventually bring them back to simplicity. But the pure soul, the earnest seeker, feels this simplicity directly in his heart, almost immediately, without any need of lengthy reasoning.

୬

What is meditation?

Meditation is our natural state, what we spontaneously are, what we have always been and will forever be. Devoid of duality, of the fragmentation generated by the I-concept, it is pure being, pure awareness, pure happiness.

This is fundamentally different from the way in which the word "meditation" is usually used. It usually refers to a technique or process whereby we can reach our ultimate nature. But, you are saying that it is our ultimate nature.

Who is there to reach anything, and how could we possibly reach what we already are? Any dynamism keeps us in slavery, in the chains of time, and postpones the moment of our liberation to some point in the future. It makes an object out of what we really are, the eternal subject. Any effort to reach our ultimate nature is bound to fail. It may leave us in a pleasurable state, a samadhi, but since this experience has a beginning in time, it will also have an end in time.

Meditation, then, does not take time, does not occur in time, but is, rather, eternally present?

Our true nature is permanent. It may, and will, call us at every moment of our daily life. It is important to remain available to it and respond with our whole being. There are privileged moments when this invitation is felt with more strength: upon awakening in the morning, just before falling asleep in the evening, after a task has been accomplished, when a fear or a desire comes to an end, when we are astonished, when we find ourself off the beaten path. We should make good use of these precious moments, especially the transitional states between sleeping and waking. If there is no compelling reason to be busy, we can live these moments completely, without dynamism, remaining open to our thoughts and to our bodily sensations, enjoying our freedom and the close presence of the peace of deep sleep.

This quiet welcoming of our thoughts and sensations should not become a drill or a habit. This would kill the freshness and spontaneity of these moments. Like a lover, we should be ready to respond to the slightest sign from the beloved, knowing that there is nothing we can do to bring about this invitation, because it comes from grace. In this way, we remain in our innocence, without any agenda, having nothing to lose and nothing to gain in the game of life.

This attitude of openness may be misinterpreted by an external observer who, projecting his own concepts, may think that a person is practicing esoteric exercises to achieve some mystical goal, when, in fact, there is nobody there, nothing is being done, and there is no goal to be achieved.

Could we go into the difference between the gradual and direct approaches to the truth?

The gradual approach is based on the assumption that we are not the truth and that we can get to it; that something which is not the truth can reach the truth, can gradually change itself into the truth; that progress can be made in time toward the timeless. Since the ultimate truth is our real nature, awareness, we can't travel toward what we already are. Any step in any direction moves us further off.

Clearly, the gradual path can only be followed by an individual entity who, getting better and better, purifying itself, weakening itself, would step by step come closer to the goal. It is, of course, a game for the ego.

It looks like the kind of progress we experience when learning factual information or skills in other fields. But, if you take a closer look, the pretense is of a slow, deliberate suicide of the ego, which is absurd.

Yes. From the point of view of the ego, there is progress toward its death. The ego can only understand happiness objectively, as a state to be attained in the future.

Would you say that in the face of a genuine impulse toward truth, one of the most effective defenses for the ego is to take that in charge, and maintain its own existence by engaging in a slow deliberate movement toward the truth, a slow suicide?

Exactly. A genuine glimpse into the ultimate strikes the whole individuality of the seeker, bringing about more clarity, earnestness, and detachment. Such an act of grace is beyond the reach of the ego. During this timeless experience, the ego is not present. After the event, the ego, fatally wounded and desperately fighting for its survival, tries to take us in again, pretending that it was the agent of the glimpse, and attempting to take credit for it. In fact, the only real service the ego can render is to leave us alone.

For all these reasons, any gradual path is bound to fail. The only agent acting in this matter is the ultimate, attracting the seeker toward his true self.

The direct path is based on the understanding that any gradual path is bound to fail. As a result of this, the mind becomes quiet, because it has no place to go. This silence, in the absence of the ego, is openness to the unknown, to grace.

ಲ

Can consciousness or awareness ever die?

Your question boils down to, "Can life die?"

The source of this question, the everyday understanding, would say yes, living things die, life can be extinguished.

Living things die. So the question is, "Can awareness be a thing, an object?"

Can it be a quality of an object?

Can we perceive awareness in the same way as we perceive an object? Can awareness, the ultimate perceiver of all mentations, be perceived as a mentation?

Of course, that is absurd, because there would have to be another perceiver.

Yes, and it would not be the ultimate perceiver. So, what we are deeply, what we feel we are, is the ultimate perceiver. We would not be satisfied with identifying our self with anything relative, objective. We don't identify ourself with our hand. We have the conviction that, even if we lose our hand, we remain what we were before. The hand and its accompanying sensations would have left the picture, but the seer of the picture wouldn't have undergone any change.

So the seer of the live hand and the seer of the missing hand is unchanged?

Yes, the missing hand is no longer felt or seen. So, in the same way that we wouldn't identify ourself with our hand, as we move back toward the ultimate perceiver (which requires a deep understanding, a thorough investigation) it becomes clear, at some point, that the body as a whole is a perceived object, and we stop identifying ourself with it. Our thoughts are also perceived, and we stop identifying ourself with them, and understand that what we really are is awareness. We go beyond any limitation, and identify with life itself, with consciousness. At that level, everything appears in life, disappears in life, and life itself is the ultimate principle everything else depends on. Even the alleged birth, existence, and death at the relative level depend on it. Any appearance, disappearance, or change borrow their apparent reality from this eternal presence, life, awareness.

ॐ

I suspect that most people rarely think about dreamless sleep. When they do, they probably think of it as a blank that isn't very significant, except, perhaps, that it is needed for bodily health. In fact, it can serve as a key to the ultimate. Can we go into this?

A blank is an object: The absence of all objects is still an object. During the waking state, when thinking about deep sleep, the waking entity projects the notion of a blank because deep sleep is a non-experience: there are no objects in it, and knowledge of objects is the only kind of knowledge available to the waking person. Therefore, the blank state is not a fact, but a superimposition that occurs during the waking state. The actual experience of deep sleep remains beyond the comprehension of the waking person. In order to understand deep sleep, this superimposition also has to come to an end. Then deep sleep reveals itself to be the timeless

104

background, our true nature. This same non-state is also present between mentations. When we wake up, we are still impregnated with the freshness, peace, and happiness of deep sleep. Before falling asleep, we feel the invitation that brings us back to our real home. Unlike the waking and dreaming states, deep sleep is not a state. It is, rather, the background of all states.

Using an analogy, if we consider faces carved in a stone, the faces corresponding to the states and the stone corresponding to deep sleep, our attention is drawn, at first, by the faces. We see only them. Taking a closer look, we notice the stone around and between the faces, where there is no carving. In the same way, deep sleep and the intervals between mentations give us the opportunity to wake up to, and experience, pure awareness. Then, looking again at the carved faces, we see them for what they really are, stone. This knowledge doesn't prevent us from seeing the faces, but, still, there is only stone. Similarly, having seen the background, the substratum (and when I use the word "see," I don't mean with our eyes, but, rather, that the substratum sees itself), when the objects arise again, they are now seen for what they are, awareness. There are no objects, there is only awareness.

Because of its revealing power, deep sleep is of the utmost importance in this perspective. Once experienced, this living under-standing, the awareness of the presence of the background, is always with us. During the waking state and the dream state we feel the continuity of deep sleep. Since the identification with a waking or dream subject no longer exists, one could say that there is no longer sleep. The awareness quality of the waking state merges with the stillness of deep sleep. This non-experience is beautifully described in the Bhagavad Gita:

"What is day to the blind is night to the seer; what is day to the seer is night to the blind."

To be awake in sleep and asleep in the waking state.

Yes. The sage, ignoring the three states, takes his stand in reality, whereas the ignorant, unaware of his real nature, takes his stand in an illusory waking state.

If deep sleep is a return to the real self, why are we oblivious of this?

We have no memories of this non-experience. In this sense, we are oblivious of it. However, consciousness is still present, aware of itself, during deep sleep. When we wake up, the peace and the feeling of continuity of consciousness are still present. In this sense, we are not oblivious to it.

ॐ

There is no past, there is no future; there is only here and now, only immediacy. Any "there," any "then," merely forms the foundation for this grand illusion within which there appears to be a past, a present, and a future. Once this is seen, once this understanding is arrived at, how is it lived, how is it implemented in daily life?

It implements itself, because there is nobody to implement it. It implements itself without our intervention in the same way as the sun rises, the blowing wind rustles the leaves, the plants grow, and our heart beats.

9

The Wonderful Play of the Timeless Now

One of my biggest dilemmas has been the master/disciple relationship. A friend of mine insists, "Never relinquish your right to question." Others think "surrender" is the ideal.

Your friend is right. How can you totally surrender if you still have doubts? Such a surrender would not be a natural one, but, rather, an effort to abandon your own concepts and replace them with new ones, those of your teacher. It would be a surrender to the new concepts, not to the truth. The truth is not a concept. It is your living reality; it is absolute freedom from any concepts. You can never put it in a cage, even in the golden cage of the words of your teacher. All you can do regarding the sayings of your teacher is to take them into consideration. If your teacher is an authentic one, his words will gradually erase your doubts. To seriously take into consideration the sayings of your teacher is already perfect surrender. It is the best you can do. Leave it up to him to do the work for you. A real teacher will always welcome your questions, at least until you have a first hand knowledge of your true nature. Then, he may choose to answer your questions if he feels it appropriate to do so. For instance, he may help you expand your understanding of the spiritual perspective to a practical problem in your life, or he may simply remind you, here and now, of the truth you have already experienced. In both cases your question will find its answer in you.

৯

Why I am having this conversation with you?

You have to find the answer to this question yourself. What is your motive? Is it a feeling of lack, incompleteness, or dissatisfaction? Is it a desire to understand?

Right now it is to understand. Do I need to have this conversation with you to understand, or is it possible for me to have this same conversation with myself? If I can have this same conversation with myself how do I go about it?

In order to understand, it is mandatory to have this conversation with yourself. I can't understand for you. If you are thirsty, and someone tells you where to find a well, you still have to go to the well and drink to quench your thirst. However, the information that was given to you may have saved you time and effort.

To have this conversation with yourself means to live with your question; to welcome your questioning whenever it spontaneously appears to you. In time, the formulation of your question will change and become more and more subtle as you grow in understanding. At some point, your question will disappear in you and leave you in your freedom and innocence.

Is it that I don't know what you know? Do you know more than I do? Is there something that is out there or in myself that I should know? Why is there this search? Who is searching? Searching for what, more knowledge? What will end my search?

What do you mean by "knowing"? If you mean accumulated knowledge in memory or skills you have learned in the past, I am quite sure there are many things you know which I don't know, and, conversely, things I know which you don't. But, you are obviously referring to a different kind of knowledge when you ask these questions.

Is there any other kind of knowledge? What is the nature of this knowledge?

There is relative, objective knowledge and there is absolute knowledge, knowledge in identity. Relative knowledge is the one to which you refer when you say, "I know this man," or, "I know how to play the piano." Most people aren't conscious of the other mode of knowledge, knowledge in identity, despite the fact that it lies at the core of everything they know. The fact that you exist is for you an absolute certainty. If you investigate the source of this certainty, you will discover that it isn't based on any of the six senses (hearing, seeing, tasting, smelling, body-sensing, and thinking) which are the instruments of relative knowledge. The certainty that you derive from this absolute knowledge is total, whereas any fact ascertained with the instruments of relative knowledge can be challenged. The experience of love, the experience of beauty, the experience of happiness are other instances of knowledge in identity. Once you are aware of this new mode of knowledge, you go back to it more and more, until you get established in it.

Now, the question may arise: Do I possess some kind of super-mind which you don't possess, giving me access to some mysterious knowledge of which you are unaware? Do I have anything which you don't? Definitely not! Like me, you have everything you need to be perfectly happy. So, what is the difference between us? The only alternative possibility is that you possess something which I don't have. What is it then?

Your original question gives us a hint. There is searching in you, not in me. What does the fact that you are searching tell us? It tells us you believe that there is something you don't yet possess, the possession of which could, perhaps, put an end to your search. Why am I not searching? Because I am free from the belief that there is anything out there that exists independently from this awareness which I so evidently know myself to be, and because I don't believe there is anything in particular in here, such as a body or a mind, which I recognize to be me, this awareness which I so evidently know myself to be. Being nothing specific, and nothing being out-side what I so obviously am, I am everything. Being everything, there is nothing to be sought. So, here's the difference: you have some beliefs about what you are or are not, or what you have or have not, while I don't have such beliefs, and stick, instead, to what I actually experience myself to be, the wonderful play of the timeless now. Since there is nobody who is searching inside me, the question, "Who is searching?" is for you to answer. This question is the best question you could ever investigate, and it will take you to the end of the journey, provided your desire for the truth is real and earnest.

Accumulation of more knowledge and skills will definitely not put an end to this search, because this quest is not about learning, but rather about unlearning the accumulated concepts, beliefs, and habits which prevent us from experiencing the simplicity, spontaneity, and joy of our real nature.

Investigating my suggestion that you are not a perceived object, not a concept, nor a feeling, nor a sense perception, will pave the way to your understanding of what you really are. This investigation has to be pursued thoroughly, both at the intellectual level, and at the level of your bodily sensations. The understanding that comes to you as a result of this investigation, the answer to the question, "Who am I?" is an experience that takes you beyond the mind, beyond time and space, to your innate beauty and immortality. In this experience, you discover you are that which you were seeking. It is the end of this question and of all questions, of this search, and of all your fears and desires.

Can you tell me what you mean by perfectly happy? I don't feel happy. That is the main reason I am still playing the game that human beings invented. In this game there is continual movement from one object to another, and the reason for the movement is to be happy. I think there is no peace or happiness in this game.

We all know happiness. We can't describe it, but the fact that we are looking for it proves that we somehow know it. When a desired object is obtained, we experience a brief moment of happiness. Our mistake is the belief that happiness is contained in the object, whereas, in fact, we already are this happiness. When the object is acquired, the desire ceases for a while, and we experience the happiness that derives from desirelessness, our true nature. Then, because of our ignorance, a new desire is born and again veils this happiness which we deeply are. At some point, as you mentioned, we become aware of the endless movement from object to object. This is a very important moment in our life, because it paves the way for the authentic spiritual quest, the quest for a never-ending happiness.

Can you explain what you mean by awareness? My experience is that I exist (body, mind) and want certain things, and that you and others are also like me. I have a feeling that I can exist independently from others. I can also move from I to we or us, and so on. Are you saying this is just a belief? Is awareness just to see, hear, and feel, or is it much more?

To whom do your body, your mind, your desires, Francis, and others appear? To you, obviously. You are the witness of your body, mind, and desires. Therefore, you are not any of these objects in particular. You are pure awareness, which is another name for consciousness, the ultimate witness of your thoughts, feelings, and perceptions.

The feeling that you can exist independently from others is quite correct. It derives from the fact that the others are not always present in your consciousness, whereas you are always present as awareness. If you think deeply about it, you will come to the conclusion that your body is not always present either, for instance, when you think, during deep sleep, or between two thoughts. Thus, you as awareness exist independently from your body, which is made out of sense perceptions. If you keep investigating this matter, it will also become clear that you are not a thought either, because thoughts come and go, and you, awareness, remain. Thus, you are not your mind, at least the objective part of your mind, the thoughts.

At this point, it must be clear to you that you are not an object, something that can be either conceptualized as a thought or perceived through the senses. That is all you need to understand. But, your understanding must be thorough and you must live and act in accordance with it.

That which you are is not a belief or a perception, whereas that which you believe yourself to be is obviously a concept, and that which you perceive yourself to be is obviously a perception. Seeing, hearing, or thinking appear in awareness and disappear in awareness. Thus, they are made out of awareness. However, awareness, your real self, is much more than the six senses, much more than the individual mind, much more even than this universe which rises and falls in consciousness from moment to moment. It is the ground which all sentient beings have in common: our timeless presence which contains in a perfect simultaneity all possible worlds, with their pasts and futures.

Will understanding bring an end to searching, and will the "Who" disappear?

When you really stop taking yourself for that which you are not, you remain as awareness. At this moment, you find the answer to all your questions and you remain as peace.

What is "Who" and what is its nature?

Again, this question is for you to answer.

Clearly, more knowledge won't bring an end to this search because the search will always be based on incomplete knowledge. Can we look at what you mean by concepts, beliefs, and habits in our daily life?

Here are two examples of concepts: man and God. Here are three examples of beliefs: "I am a man," "God exists," or "God doesn't exist." When a belief becomes permanent, it creates habits. For instance, the belief, "I am a separate entity" will create certain patterns of defense-aggression, of greed, of fear and desire.

Is everything we know a concept? What is real and what isn't real?

Not everything we know, even in the objective realm, is a concept. For instance, a bodily sensation is not a concept. Everything that comes and goes is not real. After a nightmare, the threatening dream world vanishes. Its vanishing convinces us of its unreality. It follows that neither thoughts nor perceptions are real, due to their impermanence. Awareness, their permanent ultimate witness, is the only reality.

How can we break out of concepts, since all our communication is based on concepts, and it is all in the mind? Won't the "How?" bring in another concept? What will bring about this unlearning?

This is a very good question. The "How?" keeps us in the mind, because any verbal answer to the "How?" is another concept. However, understanding is not a concept. In order to understand, we go beyond the mind. Some concepts have the power to take us to this intelligence, to take us beyond the mind. If we live with such a concept for a while, if we think about it and investigate, there comes a moment when it suddenly vanishes in understanding.

10

Real Understanding Is in the Heart

Most people, in their everyday lives, are involved in making a living, getting along with others, and through it all, trying to find some happiness. Does the non-dualist view have anything to say that would be of help to such a person?

We all seek happiness. Most people struggle to reach this apparently inaccessible goal. As a child, we look for happiness in the toy we are expecting; as a teenager, we may hope to reach it if we are lucky enough to win the next game, or have a date with the handsome boy or beautiful girl we saw on the beach; as an adult, we may think that the recipe for happiness is a complex blend of having a good job, being happily married, owning a house, having children, being healthy, and so on. When we take a global look at this picture, we see that we are in a permanent state of striving, always desiring something, always fearing something, always looking for happiness, and always unhappy. This endless oscillation between the past and the future prevents us from fully living the present reality of our life. It generates a deep dissatisfaction in us, which, if we listen to it, will turn out to be a very positive feeling. This dissatisfaction leads to questions, such as: "How can I escape from this infernal circle of fear and desire? Where does this happiness I have experienced from time to time come from? Can I be permanently established in this happiness? Can I live a life that is full and creative? How can I make the best use of my time?"

These questions indicate that we are already somewhat mature, in the sense that we have seen the problem. We have somehow understood that going from desire to desire is a dead end, and that as soon as we have acquired the desired object or avoided the feared event, we go on to something new, in an endless process of striving. When we see that, we are open to a new perspective. Having understood that the peace and happiness we are seeking can't be found in any object, that what we really desire is not the object itself but the happiness that was unveiled when we obtained the desired object and the desire ceased, we start aiming directly at the desireless state, happiness, instead of aiming at objects.

A detachment that is a natural result of this understanding then follows. This dispassion is not arrived at through effort, but rather appears by itself. The energies coming from our center, which until now were dispersed in the search for objects, have lost their external goals. They keep flowing back to their source until we find ourself to be what we were seeking.

If we can't think the truth or sense the truth, how can we possibly approach the truth?

We can't approach the truth either, because we are the truth. The entity that wants to approach the truth has to cease to exist for the truth to be revealed. This limited entity is an illusion. It borrows its reality from its source, the truth. The truth can't be felt or sensed, because it doesn't belong to the mind. Mind, thoughts, sensations appear in the truth, they have their source in it. As Krishna, the teacher, says in the Bhagavad Gita, "The beings have their roots in me, but I don't have my roots in them."

The understanding that we can't approach the truth because we are it, that the mind can't conceive, grasp, or reach it, that the mind can't perceive that which is beyond the mind and perceives the mind, is the only prerequisite for knowingly being the truth. This understanding has a life, a power of its own that eventually removes all the accumulated veils and enables the truth to become self-evident.

It seems to me that the only way we could "knowingly" be the truth is if it is self-evident. Is it self-evident?

When we use the word "truth," it refers to the absolute truth, not to a relative truth which is a concept, which can be accurate today or false tomorrow, which depends on the circumstances. Absolute truth is self-evident. It doesn't refer or apply to any object. Relative truth can be formulated, but absolute truth is beyond any formulation.

Absolute truth is the source of any deep conviction, of higher understanding. That is why we call it "truth." It gives us a deep conviction of self-evidence. If we ask somebody, "Do you know who you are?" he will probably hesitate before answering. However, if we ask, "Do you know that you are, that you exist?" there will be no hesitation in answering, because this question refers directly to a self-evident reality, to a source of absolute conviction. It connects us directly with the core of our being.

Does the fact that this is a direct and self-evident knowing mean that it has no possible opposite?

Yes. It has no opposite because it is not a concept or a perception. It is not an object. It exists by itself. It is the only thing that exists by itself, and ultimately the only thing that is: not a thing, not a non-thing, our ultimate reality.

The understanding of the non-dual perspective is the clarification of the question "Who am I?" through the elimination of that which I am not, until the answer to the question "Who am I?" reaches the same degree of conviction and spontaneity as the answer to the question "Am I?" This living answer can never be formulated. It is the source from which our certitude of being originates. These two questions lead to a single answer, the only absolutely satisfactory answer we can ever receive.

Why is this perspective so extraordinarily difficult for the mind to grasp?

This perspective is not only extraordinarily difficult, but it is impossible for the mind to grasp. However, this perspective is easy for the heart to understand: very easy, almost immediately graspable.

How do we understand anything with the heart? How do we experience that? How do we know that we aren't simply caught in another set of concepts?

The heart is the only way to understand. Any real understanding is through the heart, in the heart. We think we understand with the brain, in the mind, but understanding is instantaneous. It comes from the timeless, not from the mind. The investigation that precedes the understanding and the formulation that follows it, may be the work of the mind as a tool, as a channel, but the timeless moment of creative intuition is in the heart.

Are you saying that the notion that we understand things with the mind is mistaken?

Yes. The mind can only grasp objects, mentations. It can't grasp understanding. When the mind conceives understanding, the ego comes in claiming "I have understood" but at the time the understanding occurred, the ego was not present. Real knowledge of anything occurs beyond the mind, in awareness. Awareness is understanding. This is true of any kind of understanding, even of relative understanding, the kind that is needed to solve a math problem. However, when understanding refers to understanding itself, we enter a new dimension. Intelligence becoming aware of intelligence, understanding directed toward the absolute truth, remains with us forever. It is a kind of implosion.

ॐ

Can acts of kindness and compassion come from the ego, or do they necessarily come from somewhere else?

Real kindness, real compassion comes from the self, from our true nature, never from the ego. There might be apparent acts of compassion that arise from the ego, whenever there is a personal motivation, such as desire for fame, personal advantage, profit, or power. These are not acts of compassion. Compassion always arises from love.

Are you saying that what is ordinarily called love or altruism, the putting of another before oneself, invariably has a personal motive on the part of the person doing it?

That is not what I am saying. On the contrary, we all know beautiful acts of altruism. People sometimes risk their lives to save someone who is drowning. They spontaneously dive into icy waters without thinking twice about it. They don't think about telling their story in front of the cameras or making money from the situation. They just do what they have to do given the circumstances. Such an action is pure compassion.

So an egoless act, a totally spontaneous act, can suddenly arise in a person who otherwise lives through the ego. Is that what you are saying?

Definitely. The ego is not permanent. What we really are, our true nature is permanent. The ego, being a concept, comes and goes.

So, with a lapse in the ego, there is the possibility for the Self to act directly?

Yes. The action accomplished in the absence of the notion of being a limited thing is harmonious and originates from the wholeness of our being.

We all know people who are generally kind and others who are unkind. Are you saying that since both behaviors come from the ego and have motives, they are different from the completely selfless acts we were discussing?

Real kindness is totally natural, spontaneous, effortless. It penetrates into us directly, instantaneously, and reaches the heart. This sort of kindness may not correspond to the image we have in our mind of what kindness should be like. Sometimes, it may look like anger. It doesn't always come with a permanent smile and a soft voice. Real kindness comes from life itself. For this reason, it is perfectly in harmony with the situation. False kindness comes from an intention, from a purpose relating to a personal entity. This goal may be a worldly or even a spiritual one, such as the desire to be in heaven in a future life. No matter what the goal is, if there is a personal motive to it, it isn't compassion.

Many people would agree that kindness is not a constant smile and a soft voice, but they would question your statement that kindness might also look like anger. Could you elaborate on that?

If you see a drug dealer approaching your ten-year-old child in an attempt to sell him cocaine, you may act in a way that isn't very gentle. You may lose your smile, perhaps even your soft voice. However, this action, being devoid of personal motives, would be for the good of both your child and the drug dealer.

How would it be for the good of the drug dealer?

Facing the genuineness of your anger or whatever your action may be, he would have the opportunity to understand the nature of his act, to wake up.

Could you describe a scenario in which genuineness confronts a person who appears to be acting in a kind way, but who actually has ulterior motives? Would genuineness awaken that person, just as the drug dealer might be awakened?

Genuineness never awakens the person. It eliminates the person. Your unimpaired innocence, your non-judgmental authenticity sees or feels the motivation, the ulterior motive behind the apparent kindness. You remain non-involved, transparent. All the attempts he makes to trap you fail, and that strikes him. The natural dignity of your uncommitted attitude will bring about in him an insight about the impropriety of his own conduct. Since there is nobody in you to be affected by it, his action will be reflected back to him like by a mirror and he will have an opportunity to understand.

Then, acts that appear to be compassionate or uncompassionate can come from the ego; but true compassion is our real nature, and genuine acts of compassion can only arise from there.

Yes.

How can we help others, or can we?

As long as there are others, our conduct cannot be rooted in love. In order to help others, one should first see clearly that there are no others. One should stop projecting a "me," an "I," in the other, conceptualizing him as a person. To stop this projection, one must first stop conceptualizing oneself to be a person. Otherwise, there is always a motive behind our actions, a lack of purity. The first step toward helping others is to help oneself. The first step toward loving others is to love oneself. Real help originates from the understanding that we are not a personal entity.

Some people may be attracted to non-dualism in an attempt to deal with negative emotions which have plagued their lives. They may be beset by fear, anger, jealousy, or depression. What can you say that might help these people?

The fact that someone is looking for health is a sign that he is health itself. How could insanity know insanity, delusion know delusion? Thus, there is a certain degree of awareness, coming from his ultimate health, that commences the search for his true identity. So, it is a positive sign. He has to start from his own level, which means totally facing the current situation. There is, for instance, nothing wrong with not understanding everything that is said in the present conversation. There would be a problem if he were to fool himself, if there were a lack of sincerity with respect to himself. He has to be very simple, very humble-hearted to understand anything. He has to start with the sincerity and the absence of personal interference of a scientist conducting an experiment.

We should become aware not only of our personal motives and the way we relate to others (family, friends, colleagues at work), but also of the source of our negative emotions, the person we believe we are, whose survival triggers these negative emotions. We should also become aware of the impact of these emotions as sensations in our body. We should welcome these bodily sensations as they appear, without taking pleasure in or fearing them, and face the situation, face the sensory data coming from our body and from the so-called external world.

This investigation cannot be limited to a half-hour meditation twice a day. It must become our concern at every moment. We have to discover our reactions in daily life situations, and become more and more accustomed to a welcoming attitude devoid of judgments or conclusions. If we judge ourself or others, we should simply see it, take note of it, and move on. We can see it as a sort of recurrent bad habit. If we struggle against it, we reinforce it; if we leave it, it leaves us. The important point is to see it. In this way, a transformation, a purification takes place. Our life appears to be fragmented into various elements, such as our professional life, marital life, and individual life. Gradually, we feel the harmony that unites these fragments. We later discover that we are the unity underlying them.

If someone is angry or unhappy much of the time, why is their search to escape from these feelings evidence that somewhere in the background there is happiness, love, and health?

When one is in the middle of a depression, one is so stuck in it that the question "How can I get rid of it?" doesn't arise. This question can arise only if there is some awareness of the situation. One should first recognize this ability to be aware of it, so that there is some distance between the unhappy state and the witness . . .

The awareness of this unhappiness?

Yes, its witnessing. Otherwise, in a very deep depression, there is no awareness of it.

Yes, it is a psychotic state.

And there is no possibility for a therapeutic intervention at that time. But even the deepest depressions are states. Any state has a beginning and an end. It isn't permanent. When we see our depression, our unhappiness, instead of becoming even more depressed because of it, instead of judging ourself saying, "Here we go again!" we can see the beauty of it: "I notice it, thus I am not a hundred percent unhappy. I am not totally in it. Something in me is free from depression."

Wait a moment! A depressed person is going to have considerable difficulty in seeing the beauty of his depression!

I am not saying the beauty of his depression. I am saying the beauty of being aware of it.

The beauty of awareness?

Yes, exactly. The beauty of this something in him that is distinct from unhappiness, and without which he could not be aware of his bad mood.

So, the beauty of being able to recognize his depression as an object.

Yes. A therapist should point out this positive element to his patient, so that the latter can recognize this quality of awareness which is going to be the main, and in fact, single agent of the cure.

Thus, I would say to such a person, "It is already important that there is in you this ability to see how you feel, how you think. All you need to do is to give it more room, welcome it, allow it in, and be open to it." Once this ability has been recognized, it has a life of its own.

What you are suggesting is that the patient will no longer take his stand in the depression, but, rather, in the awareness of the depression.

Yes. There will be relapses, but there will already be a clear understanding between the relapses. In this clear understanding, the false notions, the accumulated trash will be spontaneously eliminated, just like opening a window in a dark room eliminates the darkness through the mere appearance of light.

There will also be a remembrance of this quality of awareness, of this distance, of this understanding that we are not the doer of our actions . . .

Nor are we the sufferer of our depressions.

Precisely. They are like clouds in the sky. In the same way as the radiance of the sun dissolves the clouds, awareness will be the ultimate remedy.

∾

Do you recommend the practice of Hatha Yoga, or any other body-oriented approach?

Regarding Hatha Yoga or any other kind of body-oriented approach, one should be very clear about one's goals. If the approach reinforces the notion of being an individual entity, or identification with the body, I would stay out of it. One should avoid any method based on the assumption that it is possible for the ego to become a better ego; that through body-transformation, through exercises, one could get closer to the truth. Every attempt that originates from a personal entity, through effort, is bound to fail.

There is, however, another answer to your question. Having understood that we are what we are looking for (there is only one thing, there is no plurality, and we are this thing—awareness), this understanding has to pervade all levels of the body-mind structure. In this case, as a result of this understanding, there is no agenda. I would recommend an approach based on the sensations: taking a closer look at this mass of sensations which we call the body, knowing that they are nothing other than awareness, being open to them, and letting them unfold in our welcoming presence. The energies that were tied up in the somatic structure are set free through this sensory awakening and the understanding that the world is in us becomes a living experience.

∾

What is a sensation?

What do you have in mind when asking this question?

When I examine my experiences, I find that they are comprised of concepts and sensations. Concepts, initially at least, arise from sensations, although they can also be derived from previous concepts. The basic element in my experience, if I can put it like that, is sensation. So, it is important to know the nature of this basic element.

From a non-dual perspective, there is no such thing as a sensation.

From that position there is also no such thing as experience.

Exactly. Nobody senses and nothing is sensed. There is only sensing, a non-dual experience, reality. The concept of sensation implies a choice, a distinction. When I say, "I see this object," I thereby imply a specific experience, distinct from touching, hearing, and so on. I also imply that this seeing starts at a certain point in time, has a certain duration, and ends at another point in time.

Doing so, I define limitations, such as what it was not (seeing, touching, or hearing) and when it was not (before it began, after it ended). By superimposing these limitations after the fact onto my real experience, which is free from limitations, I create this particular object called a sensation. But these limitations have no intrinsic reality, they are concepts in the same way that the tail of the cat or the head of the cat are concepts.

If we say, "Sugar is not sweetness" we draw a distinction between the word sugar, which is a concept, and the sensation of sweetness which is not a concept. What is the nature of this thing which is not a concept?

It is reality itself, our true nature. But then, as such, it isn't limited. Only a concept limits it.

So, when I experience the color red . . .

You are one with it.

It is a sensation, somehow not limited, but yet it is not blue.

It is only seeing, and after this experience you qualify it by saying, "It was red."

So sensation which is objectified is a concept, but as seeing or hearing it is awareness itself.

Yes, the real nature of sensation is awareness. We are one with it.

ဏ

From this perspective, what is the nature of feelings and emotions?

Feelings and emotions have a profound impact on our body. They are sensations triggered by more subtle mental impulses, which in turn can originate from two sources.

The first type of impulses originate from the mind, from the concept that we are a limited entity. They correspond to negative emotions, such as anger, hatred, or fear. They generate stress, heaviness, pressure, constriction, or tension at the somatic level. They make us feel our body as a localized, space-limited entity of flesh and bones.

The second type of impulses originate from beyond the mind, from our ultimate ground. They correspond to positive emotions and feelings such as love, happiness, gratitude, awe, respect, and sense of beauty. They generate release, relief, and relaxation at the somatic level. They make us feel our body as a non-localized expansion of awareness.

From your description of positive emotions leading to feelings of expansion and relaxation, and feelings originating in the ego as producing constrictions and tensions, I would think that the former are likely to leave more or less long-term traces in the body, whereas the latter are less likely to do so.

The former even have the power to erase the traces of the latter. For instance, if somebody makes a joke in a tense situation, we lighten up and relax a little, because humor is a positive emotion.

What you are describing here is a sudden upcoming of positive emotions removing bodily traces of a current negative state. I was referring more to a long-standing negative state rooted in the body, perhaps from years back.

I was using this example to show that we are already familiar with this mechanism and how it works. If we frequently experience psychological states that create negative emotions, a chronic condition may establish itself at the somatic level, in the muscles and even in the cells.

So, there must be some kind of ongoing change in structure and function?

Yes.

And this structure that has been changed over the years is still open to being removed or reversed by the power of positive emotions?

Yes, by the power of awareness. When awareness is allowed to penetrate into the realm of bodily sensations, in the same way as light eliminates darkness, it cleanses the whole somatic structure and eliminates the old residues. This process may take a while. If I have kept my shoulders raised for thirty years because of a permanent fear, I first have to get rid of the fear, which happens the moment I realize that I am not a personal entity. Then at some point, my body will send a signal, a sensation, to tell me that this defensive attitude isn't required in the current circumstances, and my shoulders will relax. Eventually, new sensations will arise from a more refined level, and if they are given the proper welcoming attention a new letting go will take place at that level.

In this way, awareness gradually pervades the whole structure and texture of the body, dissolving the somatic residues of the ego. As bodily awareness deepens, heaviness and tensions disappear. The body is felt to be transparent, empty, and at some point, "luminous." It is no longer sensed as a material mass limited at the surface of the skin, but rather as a subtle current of awareness expanding into the surrounding space, and, at a later stage, including it.

When this becomes our experience, it can be truly said that we stand as awareness in the presence of bodily sensations and perceptions, or in other words, that the world is in us.

This transfiguration of the body is made possible by the understanding that we are not a limited entity, which in turn, establishes the proper welcoming attitude. This understanding is the instantaneous apperception of our welcoming presence, awareness, which destroys the false identifications in the flames of our eternal splendor.

∾

Could you speak a bit about how your teacher was able to help you?

His words erased the doubts in my mind and left me open to the possibility that we stand as awareness between mentations. His presence made this possibility a living reality.

11

Deep Sleep Is, Death Is Not

What makes the diverse world appear as a homogeneous and meaningful whole?

It is its source, consciousness. It glues the various elements together, because two objects can never directly refer to one another. Every object refers only to its source, consciousness. Two objects, be they thoughts or perceptions, can never be put in a direct mutual relation.

If no two objects can be put in relation with one another, and only one object can appear at a time, we might expect the resulting show to be fragmented. But, it certainly leaves us with the impression of being a continuous fabric running constantly, with no holes anywhere, and not fragmented. Where does the seeming continuity of the whole arise?

From consciousness. This continuity is the continuity of consciousness. This permanence doesn't belong to the world. This becomes evident when we move from the waking state to the dream or deep sleep states. The world borrows its continuity from consciousness, in the same way as the screen is the permanent element behind the movie. Continuity, reality, being, consciousness are synonyms from this vantage point. They refer to the same "I am."

Would you comment on the Buddhist view that the universe, like a movie, appears in a series of still frames in succession? Ramana Maharshi also used this analogy. Physics, on the other hand, doesn't find anything of the sort. If there is any discontinuity at all, it is to be found in quantum mechanics, where the process of observation, of "measurement," on a physical system, seems to generate an abrupt discontinuity. The Buddhists claim that these discontinuities are there and that they can experience them. Are you saying that continuity is somehow "loaned" to something that is discontinuous by consciousness?

Yes, real continuity lies in consciousness. Consciousness is the only "thing" we directly experience to be continuous, ceaseless. Everything else is impermanent. The world seems permanent only because we have displaced the emphasis from consciousness to the objects, to the appearances.

ॐ

What is the difference between deep sleep and death?

Deep sleep is, death is not.

Can you expand further?

Death is a superimposition, a concept, whereas deep sleep is our real nature. Death is not real, deep sleep is our permanent reality.

I think this question springs from an assumption that consciousness is absent in deep sleep, due to the absence of memory. Hence, the seemingly apparent similarity: the absence of the body, of the world, of consciousness.

Yes, but what you see when you see a body lying motionless is not the actual experience of death. What really matters is firsthand knowledge, not projections.

If you see a dead body versus a sleeping body, you are not saying that the one is any more or less a projection than the other?

Of course not, but you are talking about a concept of deep sleep or death, not the actual experience.

Yes, but the question is arising from a common experience. We have no firsthand knowledge of death, and absolutely no memory or knowledge about deep sleep. So, what firsthand knowledge do we have of either?

We have a very good firsthand knowledge of deep sleep. When we wake up, nothing really changes, in the same way as the screen doesn't change at the beginning of a movie. The screen is there before, during, and after the movie. Deep sleep is constant, present at any time. To conceptualize it as a state that begins when we "fall asleep" and ends when we "wake up" amounts to differentiating between the screen during the movie and the screen in the absence of the movie. This distinction is a mere concept about the screen. The screen is always the same.

So, what is ordinarily thought of as deep sleep is every bit as much a concept as is death?

Yes.

When you say deep sleep is and death is not, you don't mean deep sleep in the ordinary way?

I don't mean the deep sleep state. We have a very good firsthand knowledge of deep sleep. We simply have no objective recollection of the experience. The absence of recollection doesn't mean the absence of experience. This is true even in the case of an objective experience. If asked, "What was in your mind at exactly 8:14 p.m. on May 17, 1979?" chances are you won't remember. However, you will have no doubt about the fact that you existed at that time. Do you have any doubt about your existence during deep sleep? Do you fall asleep as John and wake up as Bill, or do you fall asleep as "I," sleep as "I," and wake up as "I," remaining the unchanging witness of all these changes? The fact that you say, "I slept well" proves that you stand as awareness during deep sleep.

∽

What is the significance of being dispassionate in the pursuit of truth, and how is awareness dispassionate?

Passion springs out of the belief that there is something to gain or something to lose. In this case, there is a fragmentation, there is some incompleteness somewhere, somehow, there is some lack which generates this dynamism we call passion, desire, fear, and so on. However, in the oneness of our true nature, there is nothing to gain and nothing to lose. This ultimate presence has no motivation, no goal. It is totally neutral, totally innocent, spontaneously dispassionate. Dispassion is not a quality we can cultivate; it appears as a natural by-product when we take our stand in our real ground. Awareness is naturally dispassionate.

How would this dispassion look to an observer? The person would still have to meet the demands for physical safety, and react to conflicting social demands. He would have to make choices. He would still have to make a living, buy food, and pay the rent. In what sense is there no end-gaining and no goal?

This person may even appear to be passionate and happy about whatever he is doing, because he is doing it without motivation. Egoless actions reveal qualities of liberty and enthusiasm similar to those of a playful child. They also have the same quality of dispassion, because, when the game is over, the outcome is immaterial and they are ready to enjoy the next game.

So by dispassion you mean no ongoing investment or agenda, but a moment-by-moment joy in doing something.

Absolutely. Everything is the ultimate. Everything is an expression of joy. That is why true dispassion is not fatalism. Fatalism produces a passive, dull behavior which lacks freedom and spontaneity, whereas dispassion is neither passive nor active. It is passive and peaceful when the circumstances don't call for action, but when they do, it is active and joyful. However, our intimate core is not involved and stands alone in its own glory as the dispassionate witness of the so-called action.

There are low reliefs carved in the stone of ancient temples in India which represent deities engaging in all kinds of sexual activities. The faces of these gods and sages exhibit a total detachment, an absolute serenity, symbolizing the peace and the dispassion of the ultimate, while the body, which stands both for the individual and for the cosmic body, performs its spontaneous activity.

One obvious consequence of non-duality is that there are no others. How is ordinary social life experienced and carried on when that is clearly established?

We all know precious moments in our relationships, moments of selfless love, of giving up, of mutual understanding, when two hearts share their true feelings without having to use words. That is how.

But these are moments. You are saying that current is continuous. For most people, they are relatively rare moments, and most social goings-on involve a clear felt perception of self versus others.

That is true, but we know these moments and they leave us with the nostalgia of the oneness, of the fulfillment we have experienced. Most importantly, we should understand that during these moments we stood as awareness beyond all mentations. When we take our stand there, there is no separation, no David's consciousness and Francis' consciousness. This experience has its own fragrance, and this fragrance is unforgettable.

If there are no others, then it would follow that there is no morality arising from the actions of people on one another. So non-duality does not carry with it any kind of moral view?

It doesn't. Morality isn't necessary because the action that springs out of the understanding of the experience that there are no others can't do any harm. It is perfect, righteous, totally "in place." I am not saying that morality as established by religion and society has no value. Morality is useful to maintain a certain order in society, to prevent chaos. It comes from a deep spiritual insight by the founders of religions but it may also include sociological concerns that were specific to a given civilization, and are now obsolete in a different environment. Real morality is created from moment to moment. It is totally in tune with the situation, because it comes from life itself. That is what is meant by the expression, "The word kills, the spirit gives life."

When there is understanding, when there are no others, there is no person here either. There really is nobody. Every question that appears is dealt with swiftly in a completely adequate manner. The usual laws and codes of conduct that maintain social cohesion are obeyed most of the time, not because they are held to be the ultimate truth, but simply because, as a result of the absence of separateness, one is spontaneously a good parent, a good spouse, a good neighbor, and a good citizen, as appropriate to the circumstances.

⌇

What is the scope of reason?

Reason is a tool. Logical reasoning is a process in time. Even in the case of relative knowledge, for instance in science, logical reasoning in a temporal succession is not the essence of the creative process. Before we find the solution to a math problem, for instance, there is a kind of spatial simultaneous "visualization" of its various components, which reduces them to a synthetic whole (to synthesize means to put together) so that they can be dissolved in understanding, in intelligence. Notice that the verbs "dissolve" and "solve" have the same common root and the same literal meaning. If the various elements of the problem are put in the right place, the (dis)solution is very near.

We could compare this spatial "visualization" process with the solving of a jigsaw puzzle in which the various pieces are in a configuration that is not final, but close enough to their final positions to give us the possibility to "fill the gap." Suddenly, we "see" the solution, which means we see the current content of our mind dissolve in intelligence.

What we call reasoning, or at least its creative part, even at the relative level, is mostly based upon this "visualization" process. This same tool can be used at the absolute level, in the search for the truth. In this case, it is put in motion by the intuition of our true nature. As a result of this glimpse, the mind with all its abilities, including its reasoning skills, becomes the servant of the ultimate.

And reason, from that point on, would be said to be higher reason?

Right, because reason takes its directives from the timeless . . .

And takes aim at the timeless . . .

Yes, and also takes its conviction, its certainty from the ultimate. It is a very joyful event to find oneself, at last, on solid ground.

There are many approaches to the truth. It can be approached on various levels, through various kinds of teachers. Some teachers can mislead. Some teachers are not living in the truth. When a seeker is pursuing a particular approach, this one, for example, how can he know that he isn't being misled? How can he know that he has arrived at something that will take him to the truth? What are the earmarks of that authenticity?

His own satisfaction will tell him. What is the earmark that you are happy? You know when you are happy. You don't need anybody to tell you that you are happy. In other words, happiness knows itself by itself. The earmark of a meeting with a true teacher, with a sage— and to meet a sage, in reality, means to meet oneself—is joy. You cannot have any doubts about happiness. It speaks for itself, in your heart.

Isn't it possible for some seekers to be deceived and yet be happy to the point of ecstasy, thinking that they have finally found the way, when in fact they are being misled?

In this case, they are going into a dream. It is like taking a drug. At some point, they will have to wake up. If their happiness is derived from any object, there is an end to it. But, when their happiness is in their own liberty, in the discovery of your their own treasure, what they really are, there is an exhilarating feeling of space which never fades away. It is absolute.

12

You Are in Love with Love

A modern teacher of non-duality has remarked that a relaxed body is a dead body. This is a rather paradoxical statement for modern ears. In our society, relaxation is a virtue. It is sought after; there are methods that are sold. I wonder if you could clarify what is meant by this?

One way to clarify it is to ask the opposite question: What is a body full of life? What is life in the body? The ultimate source of everything, life itself, is consciousness. All that appears, including the world and the body, appears in consciousness as sensations or thoughts. So, a body that is alive is a body full of consciousness, totally open in consciousness.

This should not be understood as an intellectual assertion, no matter its value. It points, rather, toward an experience in which the body, instead of being felt, as is usually the case, as solid, opaque, heavy, dead, is felt as aerial, transparent, weightless, eminently alive. As long as we maintain the notion that we are our body, an object with a contour and a weight, we maintain its heaviness, its solidity, its objectivity. We make it inert and dead like a stone.

135

When you describe a stone to be well-defined, with a discrete shape and mass, and say that it is dead, people would agree. But, if you say the same thing about the body, when it seems to be opaque and well-defined in shape, they would object and say, "No. What we mean by alive is not formless, light, or weightless, but rather sensitivity and awareness." They would say that they can lie down and be completely relaxed, but be sensitive and very aware of their surroundings; hence, unlike the stone, alive. I think that is where the difficulty comes in understanding why, "A relaxed body is a dead body."

Before we go there, let's first understand that what kills the body is our identification with it, and what makes it alive is our disidentification from it. Going back to your question, it could be said that the ultimate relaxation is beyond activity and passivity, tension and relaxation.

This ultimate relaxation can't be achieved as long as you identify yourself with your body. You may achieve a certain degree of vacuity, expansion, or lightness using sophisticated relaxation methods. At the end you may even have an apparently totally relaxed body, a blank body. So what? You are still caught in duality as a subject facing an absence of sensations, a dead object, a dead body. Sooner or later boredom appears, followed by desire, fear, and activity.

When we understand that what we are, awareness, can't be a perceived object, we effortlessly, instantaneously, disidentify ourself from our body and find ourself as welcoming beyond activity and passivity. From this vantage point of a disidentified witness, the psychological and somatic traces of past experiences lose their potency and their virulence before being, in due time, completely erased.

Only in this manner can the total weightlessness to which I was alluding be achieved. As long as we identify ourself with a perceived body-mind, this identification maintains in existence blind zones in the body (areas which have not been explored, which are not open to consciousness) and localizations (areas of muscular tension which are perceived as being "me").

This black-and-white picture of bodily sensations is what we usually call "me" or "my body" and it is what I call a dead body, a mass of old patterns inherited from the past. If the attempt to relax the tense areas originates from the person, this dynamic entity will find new localizations to maintain its existence. The tense areas may have been cleared or relaxed, but new tensions continue to be created somewhere else, and we are still facing a dead "relaxed" body. We have simply dragged the corpse from one location to another.

Real letting-go takes place in the absence of an ego, of any dynamism. As a result, the energies frozen in the old localizations are set free and expand into the surrounding space, the blind zones open up and become sensitive, and the entire psychosomatic structure gradually returns to its natural condition.

I often feel that there must be a right way to live, to reduce the noise in my life, so to speak. Is that something that I should impose on myself or is that something that arises naturally as understanding deepens?

The right way of living comes only from understanding, through a self-correcting process. When we understand that the old ways of facing situations were not appropriate, we naturally change our ways of doing things. This change doesn't involve any effort.

It doesn't come out of the mind?

The mind may be used as an instrument, but there is no resistance. When you clearly see that it is necessary to take or to avoid a specific action, you just act or refrain from acting. Since your action or non-action comes from a clear vision, there is no conflict, no effort.

If your teacher gives you advice about something in your life (which you don't see) that needs to be changed, should you follow the advice out of trust in him, rather than because you, yourself, have seen and understood the problem?

A real teacher would not impose anything on you. He may make a suggestion, which you may well take into consideration and try to see what he sees, that you don't see. If there is an immediate danger, for instance, and there is no time for reflection, you may have to act out of trust, out of faith, and postpone the intellectual understanding of the situation. But your trust in your teacher, not in a person but in the ultimate reality he so beautifully represents, comes from higher intelligence, so that it can't be said that your action doesn't come from understanding.

Real understanding doesn't necessarily mean rational understanding. When we are moved by love or by beauty, these emotions too, even if they sometimes appear to be irrational, come from higher intelligence. If there is no need for immediate action, it would be better to wait until your understanding is complete. On a pedagogical level, your teacher may suggest a different attitude in life which would be more harmonious, and there is no way for you to really be sure about it without trying.

Trust is inherent in any learning process. It enables the young bird to take off for the first time; the young child who doesn't know how to swim to dive into the pool where his parent is waiting, ready to catch him; the violin student to try the new bow grip his teacher has just recommended. The bird trusts out of instinct; the child out of love; the violin student out of reason; and the truth-seeker out of supreme understanding, which encompasses instinct, love, and reason. Trying is part of the spiritual investigation in the same way as experimenting is part of the scientific inquiry. You follow the advice of your teacher, but you ultimately have to arrive at your own understanding.

So it wouldn't really be useful for anyone to follow secondhand advice. For example, someone may tell you that his teacher told him to be a vegetarian.

Regarding secondhand advice, you should always be concerned with possible distortions. However, you should remain open-minded, and be especially open to any direct suggestions coming from your own teacher. If your teacher makes a suggestion to you to become a vegetarian, for instance, you owe it to him to try this diet. After trying it for a while you will be able to make up your own mind based on your own experience. It is part of the unlearning process and it teaches you a lot about your old habits and beliefs. If you took a trip to an exotic country, the discoveries you'd make about yourself when in a new situation would be more important than the new landscapes you'd see and the new people you'd meet. The old habits become apparent. A change in diet is similar to a trip to an unknown country.

In terms of the original question, your answer seems to be, except for emergencies, which are rare, there really is no imposition. Everything is based on understanding and allowing understanding to act.

Absolutely. However, there are circumstances in which following a suggestion from someone you respect and trust, and postponing any conclusion, may be the most direct path, because the understanding won't be solely intellectual, but also based on experience, as illustrated by the example of the violin student. Instead of procrastinating and wondering whether following the advice would prove fruitful, he may try the grip and be immediately convinced.

What if you don't have a teacher? How do you go about finding someone who will make those suggestions, to gain understanding, and to develop the right way of living?

Let's first understand that the right way of living is not a collection of recipes or suggestions. Life is not like cooking, and books can't really tell us how to handle our relationships with our spouse, our children, and so on. The right way of living comes from a global understanding which potentially contains all the ingredients, all the know-how, that eventually will enable the disciple to be autonomous and live in joy and harmony.

This global understanding is potentially available to everyone, but only those who have reached the required maturity are open to it. When I was a newcomer to the spiritual path, a friend once took me to a metaphysical bookstore in the Latin Quarter of Paris. I was surprised to find a new bookstore at a location that was very familiar to me, since I used to walk down that street every day a few years before, when my interest for the ultimate truth was still dormant. I spent several years as a college student in this area and knew all the bookstores, or at least I thought I did. I was even more surprised when my friend told me that this inconspicuous shop had been there during all those years, adding that it was known to be visible only to truth seekers. The truth, symbolized in this analogy by the bookstore, had always been in plain sight, available to all, but only the truth-lovers, because of their "oriented desire," could recognize it.

In the same way as the compass always indicates the direction of the North Pole, so do the truth seeker's mind and heart invariably point toward the ultimate. When truth seekers find themselves spontaneously preoccupied most of the time with the ultimate truth, they should know that they are indeed fortunate, and that this sacred preoccupation comes from the divine. When they find themselves desiring to meet their teacher, the ultimate truth in human form, they should know that no power in all worlds could possibly prevent this encounter. When this desire becomes strong and steady, its strength and steadiness are signs that its fulfillment is imminent.

Your question was based on the assumption that the truth seeker, as a personal entity, is the source of the desire for an instructor. From this vantage point, one can legitimately wonder whether one will ever meet such a rare and hard-to-find master, since, statistically speaking, the odds are not good.

Fortunately, your original assumption is questionable, since the ego could not possibly desire this encounter, any more than a deer could desire a face-off with a hunter. The desire for a teacher, which is, in fact, a form of desire for truth, comes from the absolute. It isn't a thought emerging at random in the brain. This desire for grace comes from grace itself and is a promise of fulfillment. When the student is ready, the teacher is present.

So there is no lack of teachers. If there were a lack of anything, it would be of serious students. Out of the pure perfection of the absolute, the so-called student and the so-called teacher arise exactly on time to participate, through their apparent learning and teaching, in the universal celebration.

଼

I have a very taxing profession, and I find it difficult to stay on the path. Events throw me aside. For example, I experience difficulties in interacting with others. Is it possible to make use of these experiences, so that they deepen my understanding rather than take me away from truth, or do they only act as diversions?

They are here to help you, to deepen your understanding. The sage Krishna Menon allegedly considered a job in the police force or in the military as a good choice for a student of truth, because such challenging environments represent an excellent test for the degree of equanimity achieved by the disciple. It is a case of, "If you can make it there, you can make it anywhere." I am not sure whether Krishna Menon actually made such a suggestion, or if he did, whether he was serious about it, but this illustrates the fact that challenging events give you an opportunity to grow spiritually and are a measure of your maturity.

These events come to you because they have something to teach you. However, you don't have to passively accept everything. Maybe the appropriate action is to leave. For instance, if someone is abusive to you over the phone, you hang up. There is no point talking to that person. You don't have to submit yourself to that.

When I am in the middle of such a problematic interaction, it is rather difficult to remain equanimous. How can I achieve that?

You have to see the situation from your wholeness. By that I mean not only to see the person in front of you, what he says, how he looks, and how he acts, but also to be aware of your own reactions, fears, desires, bodily sensations, and thoughts.

This will bring about a positive change in you and will enable you to face situations in a creative way, instead of repeating the same automatic responses again and again. The upcoming emotions in you are not necessary. You can face a situation without any personal involvement. The situations are there, in a way, to teach you this equanimous attitude. It is a purification process through understanding.

As soon as you take yourself for a personal entity, you feel threatened, and you have to protect yourself, whereas if you see the situation from your wholeness, there is nobody in need of protection, nor is there anybody attacking you. From this understanding, an action or a non-action will emerge, a gesture, a smile, a welcoming silence, or an unexpected intervening event we could call a miracle, which will bring about a resolution.

So, people who think that work, the usual lifestyle that we need to live in society, is an impediment to being a seeker, have, to a certain extent, a misconception of what being a seeker is. Living a normal busy life, you can use every moment of the day to try to deepen your understanding.

Absolutely. The purpose of any situation is to deepen our understanding. Our existence is a constant learning through and from the situations. They are life itself teaching us happiness. The teacher is always with us under the guise of the ever-changing circumstances. We have to welcome them with the same love and listen to them with the same attention we give to the words of our teacher. In this way, the causeless bliss once experienced in the glorious presence of our instructor is discovered as the permanent background of our daily activities.

I used to think that devotion and worship were all that was needed. However, since I began delving more deeply into the sacred literature, and even more so through our conversations, something has happened, and I don't think of myself as a worshipper any longer, nor anything else for that matter.

That is good!

I was going to ask whether it would be useful for me to understand the nature of what has happened here.

If you think of yourself as a worshipper, it prevents you from being a perfect devotee, because perfect devotees don't have any image of themselves. The only object of their thoughts is their beloved. When you love, you lose yourself in love. When you become deeply interested in your real nature, you unknowingly become a perfect

142

worshipper, beyond all images. Your love for the ultimate truth is pure. It is purer than the love you have for a person, even your teacher, as long as you take him for a person, or for any other image of the truth, any personal god, for example. Your love for truth is free from limitations and from attachments.

If you identify your self with the body-mind complex, your longing for the object of your love is tainted by a secret demand, the desire to be loved, to be happy. When you seek truth itself, you aren't projecting any anticipated outcome. Your desire remains innocent, devoid of any personal and emotional flaws. You aren't seeking understanding for yourself as a person. You are seeking intelligence for the sake of intelligence, love for the sake of love. You are in love with love. There is no room for an ego, for attachment, or any other negative emotion.

I continue to think of myself as a woman, a wife, and a psychologist, and these identifications are reinforced every day through my interactions with others. I know that they are labels, analogous to thinking of myself as a worshipper. I haven't experienced a weakening of these labels in the same way as I have experienced a weakening of my notion of being a worshipper. Why is that so?

What you have experienced is a shift from being an worshipper to being a truth-seeker, which is a more impersonal position. From this position, you have the opportunity to clearly see that to take your self for a person is a fatal addiction which makes your life miserable and prevents you from being a perfect worshipper, wife, or truth-seeker.

As long as there is a worshipper, adoration is imperfect. True adoration takes place when the worshipper is completely consumed in the fire of adoration. This implies a total absence of resistance, an absolute surrender. If you surrender to the ultimate, but you want, at the same time, to be present as an adorator in order to enjoy the proximity of your beloved, your giving up is not complete. The worshipper needs to die for the final fusion to be achieved. When this happens, the notion of being a worshipper, or anything else for that matter, is not simply weakened but totally destroyed.

143

Having understood that the worshipper can't bring about this fusion, that there is nothing you can do, live in this non-knowing and non-doing, welcoming your thoughts and sensations. When the decisive moment comes, when you hear from the depth of your being the call of your beloved, make sure that your giving up is total, at all levels. Surrendering body and mind, heart and soul, let his sweet appeal give you the courage to face the imminent death of your illusions. Be bold. Take your stand in awareness and watch the I-image and its cortege of fears and desires fade away in the splendor of your eternal presence.

છૈ

You often suggest that we act from our totality. What is this totality, and how can we know that we are acting from it?

Totality means the absence of the division generated by the I-image. In this absence, we are in our wholeness, our undivided ground.

The action that comes from undivided understanding falls in the right place. When you are solving a jigsaw puzzle, looking for a piece to match a given hole, and find the matching part, you know beyond a doubt that you have found the right piece. In the same way, when you find the right answer to a given situation, you know it, not because you follow all the written "dos and don'ts," but because it is the right thing to do here and now, given the circumstances.

If I am confronted with someone who is in a position to maltreat me, and I am in a very difficult situation, are you suggesting that I somehow act without a separation between myself and the other person? It isn't easy to see how I could incorporate what looks like someone else's ill intent into me, and not separate myself from it. In fact, my tendency would be to walk away from it. How is that done?

If this person is maltreating you, why would you stay? Your decision to leave may be the right one.

144

And it would be acting from my wholeness?

Absolutely. You see the situation in its totality, including your feelings and thoughts, and out of this seeing an action arises: to stay or to leave; to say something or to remain silent; or perhaps, to offer a piece of candy to that person. This action will be perfect both for you and the other person.

I have had an experience which tells me that I am not a thing, an object, but I don't know how to further explore this experience, or what the experience even means. Can you help me?

When you refer to this experience, are you saying that this experience is no longer present?

No, I would say it is still present. It was a one-hundred-eighty degree shift. Sometimes, I am more aware of it, sometimes less so, but it is still there. It left me with the impression that I am not my body or my mind or any object. Can you help me to understand it? Where should I go from there?

Who wants to go somewhere?

I guess, whoever had the reflection of the experience . . . my mind . . . I don't know.

If you understand that you are not your body or your mind, if you see it clearly, there is no desire to go anywhere.

My understanding is limited. How can I refine it? Very often, I go back to the old notion that I am a body-mind.

In these moments, you forget the understanding, but the understanding doesn't forget you. It does not need to be refined—it is. There is nothing to add to it or to subtract from it. It is perfect as it is. Just keep it in your heart, make it your best companion, your constant reference, the standard by which you measure everything in your life. Make use of it, go back to it as often as you need. It is your best friend. It is here for you. It is you. When you think you have lost it, you are, in fact, desperately looking everywhere for the necklace you are still wearing around your neck.

I also understand the desire to be a good student on the path. This desire comes directly from truth. In this regard, the dialogue between a martial arts student and his master comes to mind.

The student: How long will it take me to become a master?

The master: Ten years, provided you practice for six hours a day.

The student: How long if I practice for twelve hours a day?

The master: In that case, it will take twenty years.

The point is that everything is accomplished in non-doing. If you try to achieve more, you wind up achieving less, unless you try to achieve non-achieving, spontaneity. This spontaneity derives directly from the understanding that there is nothing to achieve, that you are already that which you are seeking.

I understand that, but there always seems to be a desire to make sense of it. So I go to a bookstore looking for books on spirituality. How do I decide which tradition would be best suited for me to deepen this understanding, to make it reverberate in me?

There are many interesting books. We should consider them as objects of enjoyment. We should never be a working truth seeker. Let your joy be your guide. Let it choose everything for you, including the books you read. But, notice that I said "your joy," not "your pleasure." In your case, since you already had an inkling of the truth, the sayings by sages from various civilizations have the power to reverberate in you and bring you back to your source, pure happiness.

13

Awakening to Immortal Splendor

I am not completely familiar with the actual practices associated with your interpretation of Advaita, but it seems to share its core understanding with Zen and Sufism, the two paths with which I seem to resonate the most.

Absolutely. Non-duality is the core of all authentic spiritual traditions, such as Ch'an, Zen, Advaita Vedanta, or Sufism. The apparent contradictions among these various traditions are merely differences in the formulations of the same truth by various sages, at various times, in various contexts. If Huang Po, Rumi, Shankara, Parmenides, and Meister Eckhart were to meet, they would immediately recognize the common ground of their oneness beyond the mind and beyond all apparent differences.

My question regards the role of the guru in the "enlightenment process" of the seeker. I was wondering what kind of relationship you feel is necessary and/or appropriate.

The real teacher is in your heart. This silent presence in your heart will recognize the fragrance of truth, love, and simplicity that emanates from your human teacher, just as the instinct of the bee wakes up when it perceives the perfume exhaled by the distant flower. This direct recognition already contains the essence of enlightenment. This encounter is, in many instances, necessary and is always an act of grace. Without the intervention of grace, enlightenment is impossible, because the ego can't liberate itself from itself any more than a stain of ink can be washed away in a bucket filled with the same ink.

The human teacher is merely an appearance, a shadow against the background of light which is the real teacher. Anything that can be said, any conclusion that can be reached regarding this shadow will be as illusory as the shadow itself. Don't try to qualify this shadow as being enlightened or non-enlightened, established in light or non-established in light.

Simply be totally open to all possibilities. The real teacher who speaks in your heart will never violate your deep feelings, never try to control your decisions. The real teacher within has no personal agenda. This presence will liberate you from your frustration, anger, and fear, and will help you actualize the beauty, understanding, and love that are already in you. If there is, at any moment, an apparent contradiction between the voice within and the suggestions of your human teacher, give all due consideration to your teacher's advice. However, if the contradiction persists, follow your heart.

Although the basic identification with the body-mind has been destroyed in the case of an authentic human teacher, students should understand that old egoic patterns may still reappear even in such a teacher. They should welcome these reappearances with equanimity, just as they welcome the reappearances of their own old habits. The "old man" which may reappear in the human teacher is not the real teacher. It is a reminder of the fact that the real teacher is not human. The guru is not the shadow, but the light.

Who was your teacher, and what kind of relationship did you have?

My teacher is the still small voice that speaks in the heart, and my relation with my teacher is perfect love. Whenever I recognize the presence of this still and tender voice in an apparent stranger, this stranger becomes my teacher and our relation is love. However, you are asking about the specific circumstances in my case. I want to reiterate that the circumstances vary with different truth-seekers, and you can't, therefore, draw any general inference from my specific case. You would like me to describe the relationship between two personalities, two body-minds. I am unable to answer your question at the level of the shadows without going into opinions and judgments, without qualifying. Every time I have tried to do so, I have been unhappy with my answers, and now I do my best to avoid such qualifications.

I am particularly curious about this aspect of the path, for it seems that so many teachers, gurus, or sheiks, require expensive, in-person visits to far away places. It seems to make the path of self-realization pretty inaccessible to common folks.

The modern means of transportation and communication have, in fact, made these encounters extraordinarily easy. Think about ancient times when a student had to walk hundreds or even thousands of miles exposed to all kinds of dangers, in order to visit a sage. The path of self-realization is not for ordinary people, but only for those who have an intense desire for the truth. In the case of an earnest truth-seeker, his desire for the ultimate will overcome all obstacles.

I am averse to most of the guru-disciple language, although I have a deep feeling that there is a teacher "out there" who I can trust, and whose method will not ignite my cynicism.

I understand this aversion. From the vantage point of the true teacher, there is no teacher and no disciple. You don't have to take yourself for a disciple. Take yourself for nothing. That is a much better position. When you meet your teacher "out there," you also meet him "in here," you also meet yourself. Then trust takes life spontaneously, because you naturally trust yourself. There is no point in imagining ahead of time what such an encounter may be like. Simply be open to that possibility, and someday a teacher will ignite in you the light of truth, the flame of beauty, and the warmth of love. This encounter will put an end to your questions and to your doubts.

༄

How did you discover your real nature?

You are asking about the specifics in my case. Before I give you the details, I have to forewarn you that this is not a "one size fits all" path to the truth. The way to the discovery of our true nature varies from one seeker to another. It may be a sudden and dramatic experience or a subtle, seemingly gradual path. The touchstone, in all cases, is the peace and understanding that prevails at the end of the road.

Although a first glimpse of reality is an event of cosmic proportions, it may remain unnoticed at first and work its way in the background of the mind until the egoistic structure collapses, just as a building severely damaged by an earthquake remains standing for some time and collapses a few months later, gradually or suddenly. This effect is due to the fact that the glimpse does not belong to the mind. The mind, which until now was the slave of the ego, becomes the servant and lover of the eternal splendor that illuminates thoughts and perceptions. As a slave of the ego, the mind was the warden of the jail of time, space, and causation; as a servant of the highest intelligence and a lover of the supreme beauty, it becomes the instrument of our liberation.

The glimpse that ignited my interest for the truth occurred while I was reading a book by J. Krishnamurti. It was the point of departure of an intense quest which became the central and exclusive focus in my life. I read Krishnamurti's books again and again, along with the main texts of Advaita Vedanta and Zen Buddhism. I made important changes in my life in order to live in accordance with my spiritual understanding. I renounced what many people would call an excellent career, because it implied my involvement as a scientist with the design and development of sophisticated weapons for the French military.

Two years after the first glimpse, I had achieved a good intellectual understanding of the non-dual perspective, although a few questions still remained unanswered. I knew from experience that any attempt to fulfill my desires was doomed to failure. It had become clear to me that I was consciousness, rather than my body or my mind. This knowledge was not a purely intellectual one, a mere concept, but seemed to somehow originate from experience, a particular kind of experience devoid of any objectivity. I had experienced, on several occasions, states in which perceptions were

150

surrounded and permeated by bliss, light, and silence. The physical objects seemed more remote from me, more unreal, as if reality had moved away from them and shifted toward that light and that silence which was at the center of the stage. Along with it came the feeling that everything was all right, just as it should be, and, as a matter of fact, just as it had always been. However, I still believed that awareness was subject to the same limitations as the mind, that it was of a personal, rather than universal nature.

Sometimes, I had a foretaste of its limitlessness, usually while reading Ch'an or Advaitic texts or while thinking deeply about the non-dual perspective. Due to my upbringing by materialistic and anti-religious parents and to my training in mathematics and physics, I was both reluctant to adopt any religious belief and suspicious of any non-logically or non-scientifically validated hypothesis. An unlimited, universal awareness seemed to me to be such a belief or hypothesis, but I was open to explore this possibility. The perfume of this limitlessness had, in fact, been the determining factor that sustained my search for the truth. Two years after the first glimpse, this possibility had taken a center-stage position.

That is when the radical change, the "Copernican shift," happened. This event, or, more precisely, this non-event, stands alone, uncaused. The certainty that flows from it has an absolute strength, a strength independent from any event, object, or person. It can only be compared to our immediate certainty to be conscious.

I was sitting in silence, meditating in my living room with two friends. It was too early to fix dinner, our next activity. Having nothing to do, expecting nothing, I was available. My mind was free of dynamism, my body relaxed and sensitive, although I could feel some discomfort in my back and in my neck.

After some time, one of my friends unexpectedly began to chant a traditional incantation in Sanskrit, the Gayatri Mantra. The sacred syllables entered mysteriously in resonance with my silent presence which seemed to become intensely alive. I felt a deep longing in me, but at the same time a resistance was preventing me from living the current situation to the fullest, from responding

151

with all my being to this invitation from the now, and from merging with it. As the attraction toward the beauty heralded by the chant increased, so did the resistance, revealing itself as a growing fear that transformed into an intense terror.

At this point, I felt that my death was imminent, and that this horrendous event would surely be triggered by any further letting go on my behalf, by any further welcoming of that beauty. I had reached a crucial point in my life. As a result of my spiritual search, the world and its objects had lost their attraction. I didn't really expect anything substantial from them. I was exclusively in love with the absolute, and this love gave me the boldness to jump into the great void of death, to die for the sake of that beauty, now so close, that beauty which was calling me beyond the Sanskrit words.

As a result of this abandon, the intense terror which had been holding me instantaneously released its grip and changed into a flow of bodily sensations and thoughts which rapidly converged toward a single thought, the I-thought, just as the roots and the branches of a tree converge toward its single trunk. In an almost simultaneous apperception, the personal entity with which I was identifying revealed itself in its totality. I saw its superstructure, the thoughts originating from the I-concept and its infrastructure, the traces of my fears and desires at the physical level. Now the entire tree was contemplated by an impersonal eye, and both the superstructure of thoughts and the infrastructure of bodily sensations rapidly dissolved, leaving the I-thought alone in the field of consciousness. For a few moments, this pure I-thought vacillated like the flame of an oil lamp running out of fuel, until it suddenly vanished in the eternal splendor of being.

For information about Retreats and Dialogues with Francis Lucille, and for details of videos, books, and cassettes, please see his Web site, www.francislucille.com.

Lightning Source UK Ltd.
Milton Keynes UK
UKOW052059110213

206132UK00002B/521/P